So far, Jonson's claim has been proved correct: Shakespeare's plays are still performed for audiences that span the globe. **Jonathan Bate** (b. 1958), on the other hand, in his book *The Genius of Shakespeare* (1998), suggested that the globalization of Shakespeare might have had as much to do with the extension of the British Empire over large parts of the globe in the years after his death.

HAD THE HISTORY OF THE SPANISH EMPIRE TAKEN A DIFFERENT COURSE, PERHAPS *LOPE DE VEGA* (1562–1635), THE ACCLAIMED PLAYWRIGHT OF THE SPANISH GOLDEN AGE, MIGHT TODAY ENJOY SHAKESPEARE'S GLOBAL REPUTE.

So, is Shakespeare's "genius" an innate quality of his being, or a matter of contingent and historical construction?

6

If you cherish aspirations of becoming a lite[...]
than to start by reading widely in the history[...]
is, first and foremost, an introduction to son[...]
practitioners of literary criticism. Literary cri[...]

EVEN A BRIEF OVERVIEW, SU[...]
TAKE US FROM ANCIENT GRE[...]
ENGLAND AND THROUGH INTO M[...]
IN 20TH-CENTURY LIT[...]

9

Aesthetics vs Morality

As such questions might suggest, the literary critic's object of study is hardly a straightforward matter. For some, such apparently vulgar issues as imperialism and Empire ought not to be wheeled in when considering the specifics of literary value. On this view, questions of aesthetics and questions of morality are best kept separate.

THE SPHERE OF ART AND THE SPHERE OF ETHICS ARE ABSOLUTELY DISTINCT.

Oscar Wilde (1854–1900)

But can the "words on the page" of a given poem or novel really be held in splendid isolation from the text's historical and cultural reception, or its history of publication and translation, or, say, its author's penchant for producing propagandistic radio-broadcasts on behalf of Benito Mussolini, as did the 20th-century modernist poet Ezra Pound (1885–1972)?

For a literary critic, then, defining one's ob‌[ject]
contentious issue. Tracing the significance ‌[...]
in the novels of Thomas Hardy (1840–192‌[...]
study of the metrical patterning of Alfred T‌[...]
terms of scholarly rigour, but both of these ‌[...]
a critical re-reading of Theodor Adorno's ‌[...]
(1970) or an essay* on contemporary ava‌[...]

TIMES IN WHICH NATURE
CONFRONTS MAN OVERPOWERINGLY A‌[...]
NO ROOM FOR NATURAL BEAUTY; A‌[...]
WELL KNOWN, AGRICULTURAL
OCCUPATIONS, IN WHICH NATURE A‌[...]
APPEARS IS AN IMMEDIATE OBJECT‌[...]
ACTION, ALLOW LITTLE APPRECIATION‌[...]
LANDSCAPE.

Such is the scope of the field in its conte‌[...]
academic discipline that is taught and st‌[...]

There are certain limits to this book. It is a concise survey of a tradition of literary criticism formed in Anglo-Saxon universities in the 19th and 20th centuries, oriented around syllabuses that have tended largely to rely upon certain exclusions: because this book is a survey of that tradition, no space will be made for figures such as **Abdallah ibn al-Mu'tazz** (861–908) or **Lu Xun** (1881–1936), even though both of these writers were highly respected literary critics in their respective cultures.

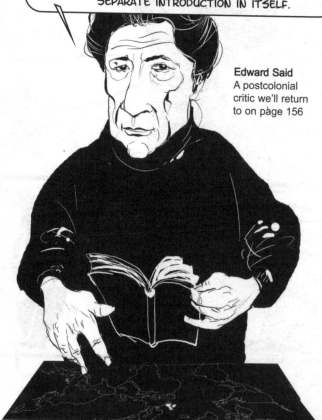

THE RELATIVELY RECENT RISE OF COURSES IN COMPARATIVE LITERATURE AND POSTCOLONIAL STUDIES HAS GONE SOME WAY TOWARDS CHALLENGING THE 20TH-CENTURY DOMINANCE OF ENGLISH LITERATURE, BUT THIS TOPIC IS LARGE ENOUGH TO MERIT A SEPARATE INTRODUCTION IN ITSELF.

Edward Said
A postcolonial critic we'll return to on page 156

A (Very) Brief History of Literary Criticism

The *Republic* of **Plato** (428–ca. 347 BC) is primarily a philosophical treatise that takes the form of a dialogue in which Plato's teacher, **Socrates** (ca. 470–399 BC), is a main character.

THE TEXT ESTABLISHES THE CONDITIONS OF GOVERNANCE FOR AN IDEAL SOCIETY OR CITY-STATE, WHICH WILL ENABLE ITS CITIZENS (ALTHOUGH NOT ITS SLAVES) TO PURSUE THE GOOD LIFE.

As the etymology of the word chameleon reminds us (Greek: *khamaileōn* from *khamai* on the ground + *leōn* lion), the extension of imaginative sympathy should also involve the exercise of **humility**. (The word 'humble' has a common root in *khamai*).

Some, though, would regard with suspicion the universalism implied in this stance, seeing instead a cover for particular interests (of class, race or gender) that the literary critic will (consciously or unconsciously) bring to bear on a text. We will examine these issues further in the pages that follow.

The Critic as Chameleon

The best way of becoming a literary critic, then, is to read widely in the work of other literary critics, while also paying careful attention to the literary critic's object of study.

ONE MIGHT THINK OF THE LITERARY CRITIC AS A KIND OF EMPATHETIC CHAMELEON, DISINTERESTEDLY CAPABLE OF EXTENDING IMAGINATIVE SYMPATHY TO THE RANGE OF HUMAN ACTORS, CONDITIONS AND MOTIVATIONS THAT ARE REPRESENTED IN LITERARY TEXTS.

Learning through Imitation

Literary criticism is a practice perhaps best learned through imitation. The German philosopher **Walter Benjamin** (1892–1940) reflected on the history of the concept of **mimesis*** (a word we will encounter again shortly in Aristotle's *Poetics*):

OUR GIFT FOR SEEING SIMILARITY IS NOTHING BUT A WEAK RUDIMENT OF THE ONCE POWERFUL COMPULSION TO BECOME SIMILAR AND ALSO TO BEHAVE MIMETICALLY. AND THE LOST FACULTY OF BECOMING SIMILAR EXTENDED FAR BEYOND THE NARROW PERCEPTUAL WORLD IN WHICH WE ARE STILL CAPABLE OF SEEING SIMILARITIES.

There are certain limits to this book. It is a concise survey of a tradition of literary criticism formed in Anglo-Saxon universities in the 19th and 20th centuries, oriented around syllabuses that have tended largely to rely upon certain exclusions: because this book is a survey of that tradition, no space will be made for figures such as **Abdallah ibn al-Mu'tazz** (861–908) or **Lu Xun** (1881–1936), even though both of these writers were highly respected literary critics in their respective cultures.

THE RELATIVELY RECENT RISE OF COURSES IN COMPARATIVE LITERATURE AND POSTCOLONIAL STUDIES HAS GONE SOME WAY TOWARDS CHALLENGING THE 20TH-CENTURY DOMINANCE OF ENGLISH LITERATURE, BUT THIS TOPIC IS LARGE ENOUGH TO MERIT A SEPARATE INTRODUCTION IN ITSELF.

Edward Said
A postcolonial
critic we'll return
to on page 156

If you cherish aspirations of becoming a literary critic, you could do worse than to start by reading widely in the history of literary criticism. This book is, first and foremost, an introduction to some of the major historical practitioners of literary criticism. Literary criticism has a long history.

EVEN A BRIEF OVERVIEW, SUCH AS THIS ONE, WILL TAKE US FROM ANCIENT GREECE TO RENAISSANCE ENGLAND AND THROUGH INTO MORE RECENT DEPARTURES IN 20TH-CENTURY LITERARY THEORY.

For a literary critic, then, defining one's object, or area, of study can be a contentious issue. Tracing the significance of references to Shakespeare in the novels of Thomas Hardy (1840–1928) might rank alongside a study of the metrical patterning of Alfred Tennyson's (1809–92) verse in terms of scholarly rigour, but both of these topics might sit oddly next to a critical re-reading of Theodor Adorno's (1903–69) *Aesthetic Theory* (1970) or an essay* on contemporary avant-garde poetry.

Such is the scope of the field in its contemporary incarnation as an academic discipline that is taught and studied in universities.

Aesthetics vs Morality

As such questions might suggest, the literary critic's object of study is hardly a straightforward matter. For some, such apparently vulgar issues as imperialism and Empire ought not to be wheeled in when considering the specifics of literary value. On this view, questions of aesthetics and questions of morality are best kept separate.

THE SPHERE OF ART AND THE SPHERE OF ETHICS ARE ABSOLUTELY DISTINCT.

Oscar Wilde (1854–1900)

But can the "words on the page" of a given poem or novel really be held in splendid isolation from the text's historical and cultural reception, or its history of publication and translation, or, say, its author's penchant for producing propagandistic radio-broadcasts on behalf of Benito Mussolini, as did the 20th-century modernist poet Ezra Pound (1885–1972)?

The book remains a canonical text in the history of moral and political philosophy, but it also contains reflections on the place and function of the mimetic arts, including poetry, which make it a rewarding text for literary critics to study. It is also, in another sense, one of the earliest surviving examples of literary criticism.

In a well-known passage in Book 3, it is made clear that poets are not especially welcome in the ideal republic.

SUPPOSE THEN THERE ARRIVED IN OUR CITY A MAN WHO COULD MAKE HIMSELF INTO ANYTHING BY HIS OWN SKILL, AND COULD IMITATE EVERYTHING. SUPPOSE HE BROUGHT HIS POEMS AND WANTED TO GIVE A DISPLAY.

WE SHOULD SALUTE HIM AS DIVINE, WONDERFUL, A PLEAS-URE-GIVER: BUT WE SHOULD THEN SAY THAT THERE IS NO ONE OF HIS SORT IN OUR CITY AND IT IS NOT ALLOWED THAT THERE SHOULD BE.

WE SHOULD THEREFORE POUR OINTMENT ON HIS HEAD, GIVE HIM A GARLAND OF WOOL, AND SEND HIM OFF ELSEWHERE.

The Theory of Forms

The decision to exclude poets from the republic is based on Plato's suspicion of mimesis, or imitation, which is regarded as an artificial, or untruthful, deviation from the true essence of things. This is based on Plato's **theory of forms**. A poet, unlike a maker of tables, for example, creates only second-hand representations. The poet's imitation of, say, a table is, for Plato, an imitation of an imitation, insofar as the table-maker's table is itself only an imitation of the essential, or divine, form of the table.

MY THEORY OF FORMS MOVES THROUGH THREE STAGES: *FORM* (UNIVERSAL IDEA) → *OBJECT* (PARTICULAR) → *REPRESENTATION OF OBJECT* (MIMESIS).

Plato also worried about the extent to which poets create inaccurate (and blasphemous) representations of the Greek gods, citing examples from **Homer** (ca. 8th century BC) and others, which might disrupt the smooth functioning of the ideal state. Similarly, because poetry stirs and excites the passions of those who hear it, poets might weaken the resolve and self-control of the city's soldiers and guardians. Plato's views about the function of poetry were thus very restrictive.

THE ONLY POETRY ADMISSIBLE IN OUR CITY IS HYMNS TO THE GODS AND ENCOMIA* TO GOOD MEN.

Plato wanted a strictly *useful* poetry, subordinating the demands of artistic autonomy and independence to the greater good of the polis, or city-state. To many readers, his comments have often seemed like an argument for censorship. They can also be interpreted as part of a more playful and long-standing rivalry between the relative claims of poetry and philosophy as a route to truth.

By contrast, **Aristotle** (384–322 BC), in his treatise on *Poetics*, defended the mimetic arts – particularly epic, tragedy, comedy and dithyrambic*, and most music for the flute and lyre.

MIMESIS IS INNATE IN HUMAN BEINGS FROM CHILDHOOD – INDEED WE DIFFER FROM OTHER ANIMALS IN BEING MOST GIVEN TO MIMESIS AND IN MAKING OUR FIRST STEPS IN LEARNING THROUGH IT – AND PLEASURE IN INSTANCES OF MIMESIS IS EQUALLY GENERAL.

Aristotle's treatise delineates the rules, derived from nature, governing the mimetic arts, including sections on the construction of plots in tragic drama and how to go about answering criticisms of Homer. Aristotle defended mimesis because it is a cause of **pleasure**, against Plato's stricter focus on **usefulness**, linking the pleasure-giving aspects of mimesis to its teaching function. Aristotle's views of mimesis, particularly tragedy and epic, had widespread influence during the European Renaissance in the 16th century and beyond.

The Three Unities

Aristotle's theory of the unities of **action**, **time** and **place**, reconstructed from the *Poetics*, had particular influence in Renaissance Italy and France. In his discussion of plot, Aristotle emphasizes the importance of **wholeness** in order to achieve the requisite degree of order, amplitude and unity.

> TRAGEDY ENDEAVOURS AS MUCH AS POSSIBLE TO CONFINE ITSELF TO ONE REVOLUTION OF THE SUN ... WHEREAS THE EPIC ACTION HAS NO LIMITS OF TIME.

> A PLOT SHOULD INVOLVE THE MIMESIS (OR REPRESENTATION) OF A WHOLE ACTION, WITH A BEGINNING, A MIDDLE AND AN END.

The extent to which Aristotle intended these remarks as descriptive observations or prescriptive rules is open to dispute, although he does offer more explicit guidance to practising playwrights.

Catharsis

Another important concept introduced in Aristotle's *Poetics* is **catharsis**, relating particularly to tragic drama. Unlike comedy, which Aristotle defines in relation to "low", or "ugly", characters, tragedy concerns "high" actions represented in dramatic form, rather than narrative form (which belongs to epic).

His usage of the term has provoked much debate. There is no exact definition, but it is generally taken to refer to an almost therapeutic, or purgative, process by which audience members learn to comprehend human suffering without experiencing it to the same degree of intensity as is represented on stage.

TRAGEDY EFFECTS THROUGH PITY AND FEAR THE CATHARSIS OF SUCH EMOTIONS.

Catharsis can extend one's imaginative sympathy and, as such, guide one's behaviour. Tragic drama, then, has *social* meaning.

In the 1930s, the German Marxist playwright **Bertolt Brecht** (1898–1956) took up a polemical, or controversial, stance against Aristotle's concept of catharsis, as part of his theorization of a politicized non-Aristotelian theatre. Brecht objected to the concept of catharsis because it presumes an audience of separate individuals, rather than seeing the audience as a political collective, capable of thinking and reasoning in response to the action presented on stage.

The audience's identification with the "inexorable fate" of the tragic hero obscures the reality of human agency in socio-economic processes.

THE ARISTOTELIAN PLAY IS ESSENTIALLY STATIC; ITS TASK IS TO SHOW THE WORLD AS IT IS. THE [BRECHTIAN] LEARNING-PLAY IS ESSENTIALLY DYNAMIC; ITS TASK IS TO SHOW THE WORLD AS IT CHANGES.

Bertolt Brecht
(1898–1956)

Defenders of Poetry: Sidney and Shelley

Brecht responded to Aristotle as a drama practitioner and a playwright. Other "practitioners", including poets like **Philip Sidney** (1554–86) and **Percy Bysshe Shelley** (1792–1822), were influenced by Aristotle's defence of the educational value of aesthetic pleasure when writing their own defences of poetry. Both were responding, creatively and wittily, to attacks on the value and status of poetry.

Sidney wrote against 16th-century puritans, defending poetry and drama against accusations of blasphemy. Shelley responded to Thomas Love Peacock's (1785–1866) essay "The Four Ages of Poetry" (1820), in which Peacock claimed that poetry was being overshadowed by science.

Percy Bysshe Shelley

Philip Sidney

WE BOTH TOOK UP PLATO'S INVITATION IN THE *REPUBLIC* TO ALLOW POETRY'S DEFENDERS "TO MAKE A PROSE SPEECH ON HER BEHALF, TO SHOW THAT SHE IS NOT ONLY PLEASING BUT USEFUL FOR GOVERNMENT AND HUMAN LIFE".

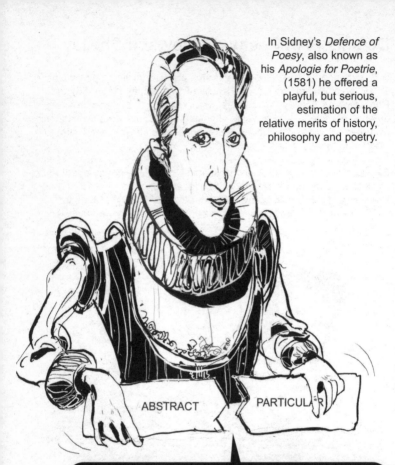

In Sidney's *Defence of Poesy*, also known as his *Apologie for Poetrie*, (1581) he offered a playful, but serious, estimation of the relative merits of history, philosophy and poetry.

ABSTRACT PARTICULAR

I MYSELF HAVE SLIPPED INTO THE TITLE OF A POET. WHEREAS THE PHILOSOPHER DEALS IN THE ABSTRACT AND GENERAL, THE HISTORIAN DEALS WITH THE PARTICULAR; THE POET ALONE CAN UNITE THE GENERAL AND THE PARTICULAR. THE PHILOSOPHER'S MISTY ABSTRACTIONS AND THE HISTORIAN'S OLD MOUSE-EATEN RECORDS ARE APT TO LIE DARK BEFORE THE IMAGINATIVE AND JUDGING POWER, IF THEY BE NOT ILLUMINATED OR FIGURED FORTH BY THE SPEAKING PICTURE OF POESY.

24

sense meant by Olney, an **apology** is a formal defence or
ation of one's position, rather than an expression of regret.

ey sustained his own
ment with reference to
ical poets, including Homer,
e, Boccaccio and Petrarch.

Sidney also echoed the discussion of mimesis found in Plato and Aristotle, identifying "feigning" (making, or representation) with the work of a poet and emphasizing poetic imitation as a means of "delightful teaching". According to Sidney, poetry can purify wit, enrich memory, enable judgement and enlarge conceit. Its aim …

… IS TO LEAD AND DRAW US TO AS HIGH A PERFECTION AS OUR DEGENERATE SOULS, MADE WORSE BY THEIR CLAYEY LODGINGS, CAN BE CAPABLE OF.

It's clear that Sidney was more in sympathy with Aristotle's defence of mimesis than he was with Plato's suspicious dismissal, which is hardly surprising given that Sidney's "apologie" for poetry was also, implicitly, a defence of his own status as a poet.

Sidney offered two important definitions of the poet. First, citing the Latin word for poets, *vates* (which means "diviner", "foreseer" or "prophet"), Sidney identified poets with "divine force", recalling one of Plato's early dialogues, *Ion*. Second, he noted that the English word "poet" derives from the Greek *poiein*, meaning "to make".

ONLY THE POET, LIFTED UP WITH THE VIGOUR OF HIS OWN INVENTION, DOTH GROW, IN EFFECT, INTO ANOTHER NATURE, IN MAKING THINGS EITHER BETTER THAN NATURE BRINGETH FORTH OR, QUITE ANEW, FORMS SUCH AS NEVER WERE IN NATURE.

In his "A Defence of Poetry", written in 1821 but first published in 1840, Shelley suggested that poetry has **cognitive**, as well as aesthetic, value and offers a particular way of *knowing* about the world, distinct from knowledge gained by reason. On this basis he maintained that "poets are the unacknowledged legislators of the world". Shelley also claimed that poetry serves a morally instructive role:

THE GREAT INSTRUMENT OF MORAL GOOD IS THE IMAGINATION; AND POETRY ADMINISTERS TO THE EFFECT BY ACTING UPON THE CAUSE. POETRY ENLARGES THE CIRCUMFERENCE OF THE IMAGINATION BY REPLENISHING IT WITH THOUGHTS OF EVER NEW DELIGHT.

The educational function of poetry is here seen to have a simultaneously humanizing influence.

Shelley did not, however, see the moral function of poetry as straightforwardly **didactic**, or moralizing. Shelley instead defended the value of poetry with recourse to some particularly arresting (if mixed) metaphors*.

A POET WOULD DO ILL TO EMBODY HIS OWN CONCEPTIONS OF RIGHT AND WRONG, WHICH ARE USUALLY THOSE OF HIS TIME AND PLACE, IN HIS POETICAL CREATIONS, WHICH PARTICIPATE IN NEITHER.

POETRY IS A SWORD OF LIGHTNING, EVER UNSHEATHED, WHICH CONSUMES THE SCABBARD THAT WOULD CONTAIN IT.

POETRY LIFTS THE VEIL FROM THE HIDDEN BEAUTY OF THE WORLD, AND MAKES FAMILIAR OBJECTS BE AS IF THEY WERE NOT FAMILIAR.

29

Pope's Criticism

Sidney's and Shelley's defences are important texts in the history of literary criticism, not least because these two poets make claims about the value of poetry, in dialogue with older **classical** traditions of criticism and thinking about aesthetics.

Alexander Pope (1688–1744), who sits between Sidney's Renaissance humanism* and Shelley's early-19th-century Romanticism, also contributed to this dialogue with "An Essay on Criticism" (1711). Pope's "Essay" in verse is written in the style of the Roman lyric poet **Horace** (65–8 BC), and offers advice to would-be critics:

> BUT YOU WHO SEEK TO GIVE AND MERIT FAME,
> AND JUSTLY BEAR A CRITICK'S NOBLE NAME,
> BE SURE YOUR SELF AND YOUR OWN REACH TO KNOW,
> HOW FAR YOUR GENIUS, TASTE, AND LEARNING GO;
> LAUNCH NOT BEYOND YOUR DEPTH ...

Pope was concerned with neoclassical principles of balance, order and decorum.

For Pope, it was important that critics know their limits. We might think of Pope's opposition between Nature and Wit as the opposition between external cosmic laws and human intelligence or cunning (also related to the "sin" of pride).

The truth of Nature can be observed by humans and expressed in clear, elegant, stylish language, but the fundamental laws are pre-given, not open to dispute.

NATURE TO ALL THINGS FIX'D THE LIMITS FIT,/ AND WISELY CURB'D MAN'S PROUD PRETENDING WIT.

TRUE WIT IS NATURE TO ADVANTAGE DRESSED.

In contrast to Sidney and Shelley, who defended poetry by writing in prose, Pope's critique of the contemporary critical milieu was written in poetic form, in heroic couplets*.

It is an essay *on* criticism which might also be regarded as an essay *in* criticism, as Pope sets out his own views of the rules of taste that direct the composition of poetry. He intervened in a debate about whether poetry should directly imitate nature or be written in accord with artificial rules determined by ancient, classical writers. Pope's own position subtly reconciled these two positions, pointing out that the ancients themselves modelled their rules on close observation of nature.

I SEEK TO RECONCILE THESE TWO VIEWPOINTS AND SEE CLASSICAL RULES AS "NATURE METHODIZED".

Ancients and Moderns

Pope made clear his indebtedness to classical writers, alluding* or referring directly to Homer, Aristotle, Horace and Virgil, among others. This practice was part of a long-running critical debate in late-17th-century France and England between the so-called "ancients" and "moderns".

The "ancients" looked to classical Greece and Rome as models for contemporary literary excellence (hence Pope's decision to write in the *Horatian* mode). You might also look to the French playwright **Jean Racine**'s (1639–99) strict adherence to Aristotle's "unities" for an example of a staunch "ancient". The "moderns" looked instead to modern science as superior to and more enlightened than classical wisdom.

Jean Racine

The quarrel broke out in France, revolving around a defence of heroic poems written by **Jean Desmarets de Saint-Sorlin** (1595–1676), which followed Christian rather than classical tradition. **Nicholas Boileau**'s *L'Art Poétique* (1674) set out the opposing case, defending classical traditions of poetry. The dispute continued into the 18th century.

Both sides were satirized by **Jonathan Swift** (1667–1745) in *A Tale of a Tub* (1704) and its prologue "The Battle of the Books", written in a style that parodies heroic poetry and depicts a battle between ancient and modern books in St James's Library.

The most notable English authors who followed classical models and rules were **Ben Jonson** (1572–1637), **John Dryden** (1632–1700), Pope, Swift, **Joseph Addison** (1672–1719) and **Dr Johnson** (1709–84).

THE

BOOKSELLER

TO THE

READER.

THE following Discourse, as it is un~ tionably of the same Author, so it f to have been written about the same Time the former; I mean, the Year 1697, whe famous Dispute was on Foot about antien modern Learning. The Controversy took i from an Essay of Sir William Temple's that Subject, which was answered by W. ton, B. D. with an Appendix by Dr. Be endeavouring to destroy the Credit of and Phalaris for Authors, whom Sir V Temple had in the Essay before-mer highly commended. In that Append Doctor falls hard upon a new Edition laris, put out by the honourable Charles (now Earl of *Orrery) to which Mr. B plied at large with great Learning and V the Doctor voluminously rejoined. In pute, the Town highly resented to see of Sir William Temple's Character a roughly used by the two Reverend C

* Father of

Pope's neoclassicism was part of a broader current of Enlightenment rationalism. According to rationalists, who valued reason above all else, nature's laws are **objectively** present in the material world – providing **archetypal** criteria by which to judge artistic creations – and are independent of the limited **subjective** "wit" of the individual.

In the "Essay on Criticism", Pope made this point by drawing a metaphorical comparison between light and divine knowledge:

FIRST FOLLOW NATURE, AND YOUR JUDGEMENT FRAME
BY HER JUST STANDARD, WHICH IS STILL THE SAME;
UNERRING NATURE, STILL DIVINELY BRIGHT,
ONE CLEAR, UNCHANG'D, AND UNIVERSAL LIGHT,
LIFE, FORCE, AND BEAUTY, MUST TO ALL IMPART,
AT ONCE THE SOURCE, AND END, AND TEST OF ART.

Another important neoclassicist was the poet and playwright John Dryden. In his "Essay of Dramatick Poesy" (1668), Dryden responded to Sidney's "Defense" and set out to justify drama as a legitimate kind of poetry.

He defended English drama, and particularly Shakespeare, against classical and French competitors, warning against an overly restrictive interpretation of Aristotle's "unities" while exploring the relative merits of ancient and modern drama. The essay takes the form of a conversation between four people, each given a classical name but representing 17th-century figures, including Dryden himself.

The English Civil War and Literary Battle Lines

As well as the literary dispute between "ancients" and "moderns", the 17th century was punctuated by the small matter of the English Civil War (1642–51), between Royalists (Cavaliers), who supported King Charles I, and Parliamentarians (Roundheads), some of whom advocated a constitutional monarchy and others a republic.

Notable literary figures played an active role in both sides of the revolution. Writing polemical tracts for the Parliamentarians, **John Milton** (1608–74) defended the legitimacy of the people's right to execute a guilty sovereign in *The Tenure of Kings and Magistrates* (1649) and *Eikonoklastes* (1649).

The loyalties of **Andrew Marvell** (1621–78) were more divided, as is suggested in "An Horatian Ode upon Cromwell's Return from Ireland" (1650). Some have read the poem as a straightforward encomium, whereas others have pointed to its possible ambivalence.

Marvell wrote that "Much to the Man is due", but his closing couplet signals ambiguity about the continuing likelihood of social strife unleashed by the beheading of Charles I on the "Tragick Scaffold":

THE SAME ARTS THAT DID GAIN/ A POW'R, MUST IT MAINTAIN.

Other poets, including **Robert Herrick** (1591–1674), **Thomas Carew** (1595–1640) and **Richard Lovelace** (1617–57), sided in verse with the Cavaliers, glorifying the crown and satirizing their opponents.

THE WORK OF THE ROUNDHEAD AND CAVALIER POETS, SUCH AS MYSELF, STANDS IN STARK CONTRAST TO PLATO'S ARGUMENT ...

POETS SHOULD PLAY NO PART IN THE CONSTRUCTION OF AN IDEAL COMMONWEALTH.

It is notable, though, that during the years of Oliver Cromwell's Protectorate, after the war, there was a revival of puritan anti-poetry ideas, partly in revolt against the refined literary culture of Charles I's court, deemed by the Roundheads to be frivolous and morally questionable.

The Cavalier poets responded with witty satires against the Roundheads. Satire remained an important political weapon after the Restoration (the period after the Protectorate in which the monarchy was restored), as seen in *Hudibras* by **Samuel Butler** (1613–80). Butler's mock epic narrative poem was published in three parts in 1663, 1664 and 1678.

IT SATIRIZES THE PURITANICAL ZEAL OF THE ROUNDHEADS IN THE CIVIL WAR BY CENTRING ON THE ADVENTURES OF THE POMPOUS, ROVING KNIGHT, SIR HUDIBRAS.

The Romantic Individual

The critical landscape in the 18th century was animated by the division between classicism* and Romanticism, although, as we will see, the neat split between these movements is oversimplified. The theories of German philosopher, **Friedrich von Schlegel** (1772–1829) were popularized by a French woman of letters, known as **Mme de Staël** (1766–1817), in her book *De l'Allemagne* (1813).

In his early writings, Schlegel set out a Romantic poetics and ethics grounded in a **radical individualism,** which laid the philosophical basis for the Romantic celebration of *imagination* and originality, going against the classicists' emphasis on *reason*.

CRITICISM IS NOT TO JUDGE WORKS BY A GENERAL IDEAL, BUT IS TO SEARCH OUT THE INDIVIDUAL IDEAL OF EVERY WORK.

Friedrich von Schiller (1759–1805) published an influential series of letters *On the Aesthetic Education of Man* (1795), in which the aesthetic is figured as a model of human freedom: the individual's creative imagination is seen as the faculty that unites sense, perception and understanding.

Schiller also looked to the supposedly organic (naturally occurring) wholeness of the ancient Greek *polis* as an ideal model of human society, set against the fragmented nature of modern existence.

Looking backwards for idealized models of social organization influenced Romantic writers in England. It is particularly noticeable in Shelley's "Preface" to his verse-drama *Prometheus Unbound* (1820, 1839). Although Romanticism can generally be viewed as a part of broad reaction against following neoclassical rules and stylistic strictures, Shelley's idealization of "institutions not more perfect than those of Athens" shows an overlap with classicism.

The conflict between classicism and Romanticism is often presented as a division between **authority** (of precedents and conventions) and **originality** (of the artistic imagination).

There are no rules or models.
Victor Hugo (1802–85)

EVERY GREAT POET MUST INEVITABLY INNOVATE ... ON THE EXAMPLE OF HIS PREDECESSORS.

An important factor in distinguishing between these two movements is their different approach to subjectivity. As we saw with Pope, neoclassicists stressed the objective nature of the external, material world (objectivism*).

For subjectivists, such as **Johann Fichte** (1762–1814), consciousness is inseparable from the external world, rather than a mere perceptual apparatus – refusing to acknowledge a distinction between **noumena** (things in themselves) and **phenomena** (things as they appear).

IT IS IMPOSSIBLE TO VIEW THE MATERIAL WORLD OBJECTIVELY BECAUSE KNOWLEDGE OF THE EXTERNAL WORLD IS, IN EFFECT, AN EXTENSION OF SELF-CONSCIOUSNESS.

In 1800, another Friedrich – **Friedrich Schelling** (1775–1854) – sought to reconcile subjectivism* and objectivism in his *System of Transcendental Idealism*.

Romantic theory, which had its origins in the philosophy of Schelling, emphasized the formative role of consciousness and individual creativity

The subjectivist position had been anticipated by **Bishop Berkeley** (1685–1753), who proposed **immaterialism**, or subjective idealism – arguing that things do not exist concretely but are "ideal", created within the individual's consciousness. For this reason, Berkeley has sometimes been described as the "father of idealism". **Dr Johnson**, a staunch classicist and objectivist, famously disagreed.

James Boswell,
Johnson's
biographer
(1740–95)

Johnson was also a key figure in the construction of a **canon*** of English literature (works regarded as especially influential or important), through his *Lives of the Most Eminent English Poets* (1779–81) and his prefaces to Shakespeare's plays.

Coleridge and Wordsworth: Romanticizing English Literature

The transmission of Romantic theory into anglophone culture was a complex process. **Samuel Taylor Coleridge**'s (1772–1834) *Biographia Literaria* (1817), a collection of philosophical reflections and thoughts on literature, played a key role in disseminating the major tenets of German philosophical idealism and Romanticism in Britain.

I BROUGHT TO BRITAIN SCHELLING'S "REVOLUTION IN PHILOSOPHY".

What is Poetry? For Coleridge, following Schelling, it meant the "balance or reconciliation of opposite or discordant qualities".

sameness
general
idea
individual
novelty

difference
concrete
image
representative
familiarity

The aspects of biographical self-exploration that characterize Coleridge's text exemplify the Romantic emphasis on the subjectivity and selfhood.

In 1798, Coleridge collaborated with his friend **William Wordsworth** (1770–1850) in producing a book of poems entitled *Lyrical Ballads*. Wordsworth's "Preface" to the 1800 edition of the *Lyrical Ballads* was akin to a manifesto for Romanticism in Britain.

> WHAT IS A POET? HE IS A MAN SPEAKING TO MEN: A MAN WHO HAS A GREATER KNOWLEDGE OF HUMAN NATURE, AND A MORE COMPREHENSIVE SOUL, THAN ARE SUPPOSED TO BE COMMON AMONG MANKIND.

The individualism of the Romantic worldview is palpable; Wordsworth emphasized the intense subjectivity of the poet's perception of the world, particularly the natural world.

POETRY IS THE "SPONTANEOUS OVERFLOW OF POWERFUL FEELINGS" – FEELINGS THAT ARE THEN RECOLLECTED AND RECORDED IN TRANQUILLITY.

Wordsworth suggested that poetry was the result of a play of thought and feeling, reason and passion.

Wordsworth's poetics of inspiration is nonetheless rooted in the faithful imitation of nature, as the poet's role remains one of "selection", rather than an attempt to "trick out or elevate nature".

In marked contrast to the elevated style of neoclassical poets like Pope and Dryden, who also claimed to imitate nature, Wordsworth argued that poetic diction (language) should model itself on the "language of ordinary men" – a choice which motivated his preference for the "popular" ballad form*.

48

One problem with Wordsworth's emphasis on the heroic genius of the poet's selective vision is that it fails to account for what the poet might exclude or deliberately overlook.

This is one reason why the verb "to romanticize" still has pejorative connotations, implying a process of idealization that is untrue to the reality it claims to describe.

For example, in his poem "Lines Written a Few Miles Above Tintern Abbey", included in the *Lyrical Ballads*, Wordsworth omitted to mention the negative consequences of the Industrial Revolution, excluding from the speaker's field of vision the traffic and pollution of the Wye Valley, as well as the itinerant workers who made a living from charcoal mining in the surrounding area.

Wordsworth omitted these features of the landscape in order to present an image of the English countryside, replete with "plots of cottage-ground" and "orchard-tufts", as natural and unspoilt.

This point has been elaborated in the work of New Historicist literary critics like **Marjorie Levinson** (b. 1951) and **Jerome J. McGann** (b. 1937) (see New Historicism, from page 128).

> POETRY IS PASSION: IT IS THE HISTORY OR SCIENCE OF FEELINGS.

In making this claim, though, some would suggest that Wordsworth obscures the extent to which all poetry, including his own, is a carefully wrought rhetorical exercise and so is never quite the "spontaneous", unmediated expression of passion and experience that he claims it to be.

The Function of Criticism

In the mid-19th century, the poet and critic **Matthew Arnold** (1822–88) was one of a host of writers who questioned popular Victorian narratives praising progress and industrialism.

Arnold's essay, "The Function of Criticism at the Present Time" (1864), was particularly important in its attempt to specify a *social* role for criticism. He suggested that the creative output of the Romantics (including Wordsworth and Shelley) was "premature", having proceeded without "proper data". By contrast, in Shakespeare's England or Pindar's Greece:

THE POET LIVED IN A CURRENT OF IDEAS IN THE HIGHEST DEGREE ANIMATING AND NOURISHING TO THE CREATIVE POWER; SOCIETY WAS, IN THE FULLEST MEASURE, PERMEATED BY FRESH THOUGHT, INTELLIGENT AND ALIVE. AND THIS STATE OF THINGS IS THE TRUE BASIS FOR THE CREATIVE POWER'S EXERCISE, IN THIS IT FINDS ITS DATA, ITS MATERIALS, TRULY READY FOR ITS HAND.

This led Arnold to assert the importance of the critic's function in clearing the way for great creative epochs by trying to find the best ideas through "free disinterested play of mind". Arnold argued that the critical faculty "is of a lower rank than the creative", but nonetheless asserted the importance of criticism.

[CRITICISM TRIES] TO KNOW THE BEST THAT IS KNOWN AND THOUGHT IN THE WORLD, IRRESPECTIVE OF PRACTICE, POLITICS AND EVERYTHING OF THAT KIND.

For Arnold, it was particularly important that the critic should rise above the "rush and roar" of practical life, maintaining a cultivated detachment from the narrow prejudices of religious sect and political party. The ideal critical stance, for Arnold, is that of **disinterestedness** – meaning impartiality, rather than a lack of interest.

Arnold is often held up as an example of liberal humanism, but some 20th-century critics accused him of naivety, pointing out that the ideal of disinterestedness could instead convey a false impression that the class interests of the mid-Victorian bourgeoisie were universal. Arnold's ideal of criticism was certainly not without a political agenda.

Arnold viewed **culture** as a means of staving off social anarchy in a society in which religious values were subjected to the pressures of new scientific narratives of evolution. (Charles Darwin's *Origin of Species* had been published in 1859.) It is the critic's role to disseminate this culture of the best that is thought and known as widely as possible.

THROUGH CULTURE SEEMS TO LIE OUR WAY, NOT ONLY TO PERFECTION, BUT EVEN TO SAFETY.

Arnold's defence of **Hellenism** (the intellectual culture of ancient Greece) in his influential book *Culture and Anarchy* (1869) casts him very much in the mould of a classicist. His attempt to "Hellenize" English culture was aimed specifically at the philistine middle class, who had risen to a position of social and economic dominance in the wake of the Industrial Revolution, but who he felt lacked the cultural sophistication, once identified with the aristocracy, necessary to ensure social cohesion.

THE PURSUIT OF CULTURE WAS ONE RESPONSE TO THE "MELANCHOLY, LONG, WITHDRAWING ROAR" OF RELIGIOUS FAITH. IT ALSO ACTED AS A KIND OF SOCIAL GLUE, BINDING TOGETHER OPPOSING CLASSES.

The Development of "English Literature" as a Discipline

Arnold was writing at the time when English Literature began to be taken seriously as an academic discipline. At Oxford, the first Professorship of Poetry dated back to 1708, but it was a part-time position, requiring only three lectures per year. Arnold held the post from 1857–67.

The position of Regius Chair of Rhetoric and Belles Lettres, the first of its kind, was established at the University of Edinburgh in 1762 and was first held by **Reverend Hugh Blair** (1718–1800).

The gradual metamorphosis of "Belles Lettres" into "English Literature" was a 19th-century phenomenon. When University College was founded in London in 1826, English Literature was offered as a subject from 1828 and the first Professor of English was appointed in 1829. Initially, however, literature simply provided examples for the study of linguistics, much as previous students of Rhetoric had studied the rules of composition.

When Queen Victoria founded a Regius Chair at the University of Glasgow in 1861 its title was "English Language and Literature". **John Nichol** (1833–94) was the first to occupy the post.

The name of the Edinburgh Chair had been changed to "English Language and Literature" in 1858, at the request of **William Edmondstoune Aytoun** (1813–65), who held the post from 1845 to 1865.

Hugh Blair's *Lectures on Belles Lettres and Rhetoric* (1783) focused heavily on rules of classical rhetoric – teaching students how to write well.

William Aytoun's teaching, on the other hand, covered the chronological spread of the English literary tradition, alongside topics including Roman literature, popular ballads, language, style and versification.

John Nichol
(1833–94)

In the middle of the 19th century a distinctive discipline of English Literature began to emerge.

F.D. Maurice (1805–72), the Christian socialist and Professor of English History and Literature at King's College London, argued that English Literature had an important role to play in securing social harmony. Literature, he argued, would "emancipate us from the notions and habits which are peculiar to our own age". In focusing on literary works as a repository of timeless truths and spiritual values, Maurice anticipated another of Arnold's key concepts: the **touchstone**.

THERE CAN BE NO MORE USEFUL HELP FOR DISCOVERING WHAT POETRY BELONGS TO THE CLASS OF THE TRULY EXCELLENT THAN TO HAVE ALWAYS IN ONE'S MIND LINES AND EXPRESSIONS OF THE GREAT MASTERS.

Subsequent critics have tended to be more sceptical, regarding Arnold's claims about trans-historical value as an ideological exercise in (secular) canon-building.

Attacks on a Professional Literary Discipline

In the late 19th century, there was something of a reaction against the professionalization of literary culture. Commenting on the endowment of a Professorship of English Literature at the University of Oxford in 1886, the poet and revolutionary socialist **William Morris** (1834–96) asserted that:

> THE RESULT WOULD BE MERELY VAGUE TALK ABOUT LITERATURE, WHICH WOULD TEACH NOTHING. EACH SUCCEEDING PROFESSOR WOULD STRIVE TO OUTDO HIS PREDECESSOR IN "ORIGINALITY" ON SUBJECTS WHEREON NOTHING REMAINS TO BE SAID. HYPER-REFINEMENT AND PARADOX WOULD BE THE ORDER OF THE DAY.

Morris's remarks were motivated by an anxiety about the specialization of literary criticism as a narrow academic discipline, which would threaten the democratization of artistic and cultural knowledge.

WHAT'S SO BAD ABOUT HYPER-REFINEMENT ANYWAY?

Belles Lettres (literally "beautiful writing") is apt to conjure images of gentlemen-scholars drinking port in oak-panelled rooms.

English Literature has (mostly) different connotations, not least because it suggests a *national* literary tradition, requiring commentary and elucidation.

While the **utility** of literary studies is less apparent compared to subjects such as medicine and engineering, we might think back to Aristotle's account of **pleasure** as valuable in itself – an idea echoed by late-19th-century aesthetes – and to the educational importance of mimesis.

If English Literature belongs to the Humanities, then it could be defined (expansively) as the study of *what it means to be human*. Spending time in the company of Shakespeare, say, will lead you to think about this differently from those who learn about internal organs.

THIS, AT LEAST, IS A CLASSIC LIBERAL HUMANIST JUSTIFICATION FOR THE HUMANITIES.

In a society where the experience of work is, for many, one of alienation and disaffection, it might seem odd that a small group of literary professionals could derive *pleasure* from the study of literature as a means of paying the rent. This is the dilemma of the academic specialist in literature.

THE PROFESSIONAL LITERARY CRITIC IS HAUNTED BY THE SPECTRE OF THE LEISURED MAN OF LETTERS.

Surely reading novels, poems and plays is what "gentlemen" do in their *spare* time? To do so for a living could seem vulgar, frivolous or, worse, an unjustifiable drain on "national resources". Besides, what is the knowledge component in literary interpretation? What is being *taught*? These are some of the objections that literary criticism continues to face as an academic discipline.

THE MOST UNFAILING HERALD, COMPANION AND FOLLOWER OF THE AWAKENING OF A GREAT PEOPLE TO WORK A BENEFICIAL CHANGE IN OPINION OR INSTITUTION, IS POETRY ... IT PURGES FROM OUR INWARD SIGHT THE FILM OF FAMILIARITY WHICH OBSCURES US FROM THE WONDER OF OUR BEING.

Shelley's assertion might seem less compelling as a justification for the study of poetry when delivered to an audience of those who hold fast to common-sense opinions and profess loyalty to state institutions (such as politicians). But it is a justification.

The anxiety about needing to justify literary study continues today, and affects the Humanities more broadly. This hasn't been helped by the onset of a crisis of neoliberal capitalism after the Great Crash of 2008, which has intensified the "melancholy, long, withdrawing roar" of public funding for higher education, particularly in the arts and humanities.

Cardinal John Henry Newman (1801–90) delivered a series of lectures, published as *The Idea of a University* (1852), defending knowledge as an end to be pursued *for its own sake*, in opposition to any more utilitarian aim of economic gain or enhanced competitiveness. He identified the "function" of the university with "intellectual culture".

KNOWLEDGE IS CAPABLE OF BEING ITS OWN END.

The current pressure on many universities to serve governmental economic and business objectives threatens to undermine the intellectual integrity and independence of academic disciplines. The implicit vocational drift threatens to reduce a many-sided subject like literary criticism to a course in language skills.

Walter Benjamin suggested, in "The Life of Students" (1915), that academic study shouldn't be seen (and therefore valued) only as a stepping stone to the world of work.

CRITICISM IS LARGELY FUNCTIONLESS, EXCEPT FOR ITS ENHANCEMENT OF OUR ABILITY TO UNDERSTAND GREAT THOUGHT AND ACQUIRE KNOWLEDGE.

Arnold's formulation was taken up by later writers, including the Irish playwright and radical **Oscar Wilde**, who was certainly no stranger to hyper-refinement, and the American poet **T.S. Eliot** (1888–1965). In 1890, Wilde published an essay in the form of a Socratic dialogue, entitled "The True Function and Value of Criticism, with Some Remarks on the Importance of Doing Nothing: A Dialogue". Eliot borrowed Arnold's title, "The Function of Criticism" (1923), for an essay that formed part of an ongoing disagreement with the Romantic critic John Middleton Murry.

Aestheticism

The two characters in Wilde's dialogue, Gilbert and Ernest, engage in a discussion that elucidates the philosophy of aestheticism*, which Wilde had encountered in the work of the French novelist **Théophile Gautier** (1811–72), and in the teaching of the Oxford critic and essayist **Walter Horatio Pater** (1839–94).

Wilde echoed Arnold's emphasis on "disinterested curiosity" as a modus operandi for criticism, reiterating the classical distinction between active and contemplative kinds of life: the public life of social responsibility versus the life of study, or contemplation, removed from social duty. Wilde identified the aesthetic with the contemplative life. Aesthetics was thus seen as being entirely separate from the sphere of ethical imperative and moral purpose.

ACTION OF EVERY KIND BELONGS TO THE SPHERE OF ETHICS. THE AIM OF ART IS SIMPLY TO CREATE A MOOD.

Aestheticism was a culmination of the anti-utilitarian spirit of the Romantic movement and the Victorian social criticism of Arnold and John Ruskin (1819–1900). But, unlike their predecessors, aesthetes denied any connection between art and morality or social concern.

Pater's "Conclusion" to his *Studies in the History of the Renaissance* (1873) was an important statement of fin de siècle aestheticism, which elevated the pursuit of ephemeral, sensuous experience and the "inward world of thought and feeling" as the highest purpose in life.

Pater's elevation of immediate sensuous experience proved controversial enough to lead him to omit the conclusion from the second edition of *The Renaissance*. Pater seemed to have left the soul out of his account of human existence – scandalous in late Victorian Britain.

Walter Pater

Pater looked to the poetry of **Algernon Charles Swinburne** (1837–1909) and the early poems of William Morris as expressions of his aesthetic philosophy. Wilde went further and *embodied* aestheticism in his ostentatious cultivation of a bohemian public persona, replete with green carnations and Egyptian cigarettes.

Thinking back to the distinction between Plato's and Aristotle's theories of mimesis, it is clear that Pater and Wilde are distant inheritors of the Aristotelian valorization of aesthetic pleasure. However, whereas Aristotle and later defenders of poetry emphasized the educational (and sometimes moral) value of pleasure, fin de siècle aesthetes sought pleasure purely for its own sake, denying all notions of utility and asserting the importance of *doing nothing*.

The Critic as Artist

Wilde claimed an aesthetic value for criticism arguing, through the character of Gilbert, that:

CRITICISM IS ITSELF AN ART [AND] IS REALLY CREATIVE IN THE HIGHEST SENSE OF THE WORD.

Wilde argued that criticism is "the record of one's own soul", emphasizing bohemian self-cultivation of an aesthetic temperament and taste. T.S. Eliot echoed this view of the creative role of criticism in the last section of "The Function of Criticism" (1923), offering a more explicit retort to Arnold's strict division between the creative and critical faculties.

T.S. Eliot: The Poet as Critic

Writing in the wake of the chaos and destruction of WWI, when liberal-humanist (or Arnoldian) assumptions about the intrinsic value of culture began to seem hopelessly naive, Eliot tried to recuperate a sense of allegiance to tradition and order.

In "Tradition and the Individual Talent" (1919), Eliot offered a vision of the literary canon in which great writers of the past and present formed and continuously re-formed an order of literary merit.

Eliot also attacked the Romantic valorization of the poet's individual genius and originality. He compared the process of poetic composition to a chemical reaction in which a shred of platinum acts as a **catalyst**, causing oxygen and sulphur dioxide to produce sulphuric acid.

THE POET'S MIND IS LIKE THE FILAMENT OF PLATINUM.

This striking scientific analogy cuts against Wordsworth's Romantic humanism. The poet's mind, for Eliot, is a receptacle for feelings, phrases and images that remain in storage until these elements unite to form a poetic compound.

Eliot's idiosyncratic view of literary tradition and inheritance devalued originality and inspiration (as praised by Wordsworth) and argued instead that an understanding of tradition can only be obtained by "great labour" and the honing of historical awareness. In the "Function of Criticism", he opened with a quotation from his earlier essay, which encapsulates his exacting critical outlook:

The existing monuments of a literary tradition form an ideal order among themselves, which is modified by the introduction of the new (the really new) work of art among them. The existing order is complete before the new work arrives; **for order to persist after the supervention of novelty, the whole existing order must be, if ever so slightly, altered.**

Compared to the revolutionary aspirations of the young Wordsworth, or Shelley, Eliot's account of the "supervention of novelty" can seem particularly conservative and cautious. Where it becomes most interesting is in the practical application of this principle. In taking a critical stance on the Romantic valorization of originality and the "Inner Voice", Eliot arrived at a poetics of self-negation.

Criticism, for Eliot, involves the interpretation of works of art as well as the "correction of taste". He argued that:

THE CRITIC'S LABOUR IS AS IMPORTANT, IF NOT MORE SO, THAN THE ARTIST'S FLASH OF ENTHUSED INSPIRATION.

His own critical writing focused heavily on Elizabethan dramatists, including Shakespeare, Ben Jonson, **Christopher Marlowe** (1564– 93) and **Thomas Middleton** (1580–1627).

Modernism

Eliot was one of the most prominent **modernist** writers in England, whose poetry radically challenged inherited stylistic and literary norms.

Virginia Woolf (1882–1941), another prominent modernist and part of the Bloomsbury Group of writers, artists and intellectuals, made similarly experimental new departures in the novel. Her novels, including *Mrs Dalloway* (1925) and *To the Lighthouse* (1927), broke with the conventions of Victorian realism, disrupting the linear, chronological sequencing of plot to explore new ways of representing the interior world of human consciousness and feeling.

Modernism is something of a suitcase concept: much can be made to fit into it. It describes a literary and artistic movement of the late 19th and early 20th century, and contains many subgroups (e.g. Imagism, Surrealism). It is identified with literary and formal experimentation, challenges to established taste, traditions and conventions, and the discovery of novel ways of comprehending the human condition.

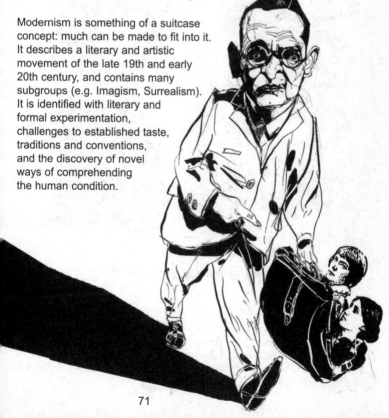

Woolf and the Struggle of the Female Author

In 1929, Woolf published an important book-length critical essay, *A Room of One's Own* in which she pointed to ways that female writers had been largely excluded from the creative and critical tradition of English Literature.

Her fictional character, Judith Shakespeare – William's sister – is designed to illustrate the way in which a woman with Shakespeare's literary talents would have been denied the chance to realize her creative potential because social convention prevented women's access to education and a room in which to write. Judith Shakespeare typifies the social inequality that exists between men and women in patriarchal society.

You might have noticed that almost all of the writers discussed so far have been men. There had, of course, been female writers and critics before this point, but part of Woolf's argument concerns the way in which patriarchal, or male-dominated, society acted to marginalize and stifle women's voices.

You might think of the Victorian novelist **Mary Ann Evans** (1819–80), who adopted the male pen name "George Eliot" in order to ensure a serious reception for her novels in an age when female writers were usually associated with the less reputable romance genre.

Similarly, **Charlotte Brontë** (1816–55) published *Jane Eyre* (1847) under the pseudonym "Currer Bell", and her sister, **Emily Brontë** (1818–48), published her only novel *Wuthering Heights* (1847) under the pen name "Ellis Bell".

Woolf's intervention helped pave the way for a re-conceptualization of the discursive boundaries of the critical tradition, or canon, helping to create and foster a cultural and intellectual milieu in which the voices of female writers could be recovered and studied.

Her own critical writings were bound up with wider social and political change. *A Room of One's Own*, for instance, appeared several years after the Suffragettes' campaign for women's right to vote had begun to influence wider public consciousness.

Woolf's critical writing is, accordingly, one of the most important early examples of **feminist criticism** (see from page 135), although her contribution to literary criticism and critical theory is not reducible to just this.

A Room of One's Own was based on lectures delivered by Woolf in October 1928 at Newnham and Girton, two Cambridge colleges that, at the time, were women's colleges, as Newnham still is today.

Woolf's narrator, Mary Beton, visits an imaginary university, Oxbridge, and the British Museum, where she encounters numerous vestiges of male privilege and patriarchal prejudice. The book's introduction contains a striking recognition:

This independence remains problematic in that only a certain class of women could afford to be financially self-sufficient. Mary Beton, for example, enjoyed a legacy of £500 a year, bequeathed to her by her aunt. She viewed this as more significant than the act of Parliament that granted the vote to women.

You might also have noticed that the majority of the writers discussed so far, with the possible exception of Samuel Johnson, Plato and Aristotle, are primarily remembered (and studied) for their work as poets, novelists and playwrights. Their critical writings which have been surveyed here could seem like a mere outgrowth of their wider oeuvres*, were it not for the fact that these documents, taken together, constitute a major genre in and of itself.

ALTHOUGH WILDE AND ELIOT WOULD ARGUE THAT THERE ARE, IN FACT, NO FIXED GENERIC DISTINCTIONS BETWEEN CRITICAL AND CREATIVE WRITING.

The brief outline offered in this book suggests some of the major contours of the tradition of literary criticism, which has frequently involved polemical and antagonistic interventions in the midst of wider cultural and literary debates and controversies.

Some 20th-Century Approaches: Three Types of Formalism

By contrast, the writers discussed next are primarily remembered (and studied) for their work as literary critics, even though some of them also wrote poetry. These writers were key figures in the consolidation of literary criticism as an academic discipline in the early 20th century.

The three critical trends surveyed here hardly belong to a homogeneous set, but their shared focus on the specificity of the literary text, rather than wider context, and their close attention to form, situates them in the same extended family of **formalism**.

Practical Criticism

Practical criticism is a method of interpreting and scrutinizing texts pioneered by **I.A. Richards** (1893–1979) and colleagues in the Cambridge Faculty of English in the 1920s and 1930s. The Faculty was relatively young (established in 1911), which allowed its members to develop a new approach to literary criticism.

PRACTICAL CRITICISM INVOLVES CLOSE READING OF THE "WORDS ON THE PAGE" IN ABSTRACTION FROM WIDER CONTEXTUAL AND HISTORICAL INFORMATION – A METHOD OF READING THAT ENCOURAGES CAREFUL ATTENTION TO THE TECHNICAL MATTERS OF FORM, RHYTHM AND STYLE.

Richards outlined the guiding principles in *Practical Criticism: A Study of Literary Judgement* (1929), detailing a series of "experiments" in which undergraduates and other interested participants were presented with and asked to comment on a number of poems that were shorn of any reference to the author's identity.

The anonymity of the material was designed to provoke liberty of expression and the results of the "experiments" were often surprising: a "canonical" poet like John Donne (1572–1631), for example, was reprimanded for his sonnet "At the round earth's imagin'd corners, blow", published in 1633.

Richards listed stock responses, sentimentality, inhibition and basic incomprehension among the various errors made by his willing guinea pigs, whose reflections he quotes with varying degrees of wry amusement and ironic censure.

Richards' methodology implied a claim to empirical and **scientific objectivity**, recalling Eliot's assertion of "depersonalization" as a process by which "art may be said to approach the condition of a science". But the extent to which Richards was, consciously or unconsciously, guiding the responses of his participants remains a matter of dispute. This is what an anthropologist might describe as the problem of participant observation.

80

The claim of critics such as Richards to scientific objectivity has sometimes been viewed as an unconscious anxiety to establish the respectability of a relatively young academic discipline by imitating the methodologies of more established disciplines in the natural sciences.

A recent turn in literary criticism towards cognitive sciences (including neuroscience) can be viewed in light of Richards' attempt. This latest turn, however, has been at least partly motivated by the scramble for limited public funding in a system that prioritizes the more immediately obvious social utility of the sciences.

Richards' *Principles of Literary Criticism* (1924) is another significant attempt to **systematize** the study of literature. Richards discusses concepts including irony and balance, as well as offering ways of differentiating between poetic and other kinds of language.

William Empson (1906–84), who had previously trained as a mathematician, was a student of Richards in the Cambridge English Faculty. Empson's *Seven Types of Ambiguity* (1930) was an influential example of the practice of close reading, or the critical practice of practical criticism.

The seven types of ambiguity arise when:

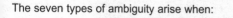

1. A detail is effective in several ways at once

2. Two or more alternative meanings resolve into one

3. Two apparently unconnected meanings are given simultaneously

4. Alternative meanings combine to make clear a complicated state of mind in the author

5. Fortunate confusion occurs, i.e. the author discovers his idea in the act of writing or doesn't hold the idea all in mind at once

6. What is said is contradictory or irrelevant, and the reader is forced to invent interpretations

7. The author's mind is divided, thus offering a full contradiction.

Another influential exponent of practical criticism was **F.R. Leavis** (1895–1978). Leavis placed much more emphasis on criticism as a **moral activity** (more than just the words on the page). For this reason, he is sometimes likened to Matthew Arnold.

His book *The Great Tradition* (1948) sought to identify the major documents of the English literary canon. Documenting the canon is a necessarily exclusive and thus problematic exercise.

Leavis was critical of Victorian poetry, which he excluded from the canon, instead locating the main stream of English poetry in a line running through Donne, Pope, Johnson and T.S. Eliot. Milton was another notable exclusion. In fiction, Leavis saw the Tradition (with a capital T) embodied in the writings of Jane Austen (1775–1817), George Eliot, Henry James (1843–1916) and Joseph Conrad (1857–1924).

In the 1950s, a dispute broke out between Leavis and the Oxford-based literary scholar **F.W. Bateson** (1901–78). Bateson was founding editor of the journal *Essays in Criticism*, whereas Leavis was aligned with the *Scrutiny* journal. Their disagreement was indicative of a sharp divergence about ways of assessing literary value.

Bateson argued for a more rigorous approach, grounded in scholarly knowledge, which, he thought, could lead to "objective" (and, therefore, authoritative) criticism. Leavis replied by pointing out that the relationship between poem and "social context" is not so straightforward.

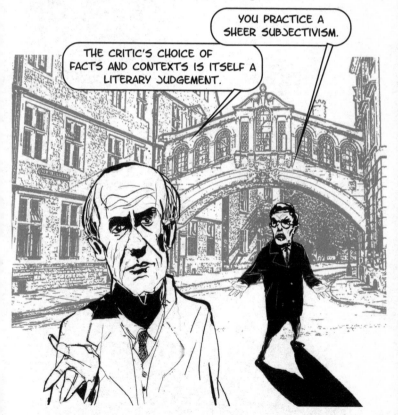

Today, practical criticism is a skill all students of literature will bring to bear in the course of their studies. The close reading of texts is the bedrock of all literary interpretation, although many students (and professional critics) will now combine practical criticism with wider reflections.

Practical criticism can now be seen as the starting point for a critical reading of a literary work, belonging among a set of critical practices that are also informed by contextual, theoretical and interdisciplinary material.

New Criticism

Eliot's and Richards' influence spread to the USA, consolidating the establishment of a school of criticism that would dominate American universities for much of the 20th century.

The New Criticism, as it was known, refers to a particular (ideological) way of reading texts, a kind of formalism that stressed the virtues of close reading, encouraging an aesthetic attitude in which a poem was best approached as a self-contained object, rather than an expression of external historical or biographical material. Many of the movement's adherents carried over the critical principles they had encountered in Richards' writings.

The movement gathered pace in the 1930s, but it wasn't until 1941 that **John Crowe Ransom** (1888–1974) published *The New Criticism*, which critically engaged with the work of Eliot, Richards and Empson.

At Vanderbilt University Ransom met **Cleanth Brooks** (1906–94), **Allen Tate** (1899–1979) and **Robert Penn Warren** (1905–89). This informal group of New Critics, sometimes called the Southern Agrarians, espoused the broadly traditionalist values of the Old South, against the industrializing impulse of the North. Brooks and Warren co-founded *The Southern Review* in 1935, a journal that proved to be an important mouthpiece of the New Criticism.

Brooks' collection of essays *The Well-Wrought Urn: Studies in the Structure of Poetry* (1947), like Empson's *Seven Types of Ambiguity*, is a celebrated example of the critical practice of close reading. Brooks strongly disagreed with the idea that a poem's "meaning" could be paraphrased in prose.

THIS WOULD DO VIOLENCE TO THE IRREDUCIBLE SPECIFICITY OF POETIC LANGUAGE.

The prioritization of careful textual analysis made poetry's relationship to real social and historical practices seem indistinct. The figure of the author, too, was drastically reduced in significance.

In 1946, **William K. Wimsatt** (1907–75) and **Monroe Beardsley** (1915–85), who were both aligned with New Criticism, collaborated on an essay "The Intentional Fallacy", in which they argued that critics who sought to discover an author's **intentions** as a key to decoding a literary work were pursuing an irrelevant and misguided line of enquiry, not least because such authorial intentions are unavailable to the critic.

A POEM DOES NOT COME INTO EXISTENCE BY ACCIDENT. THE WORDS OF A POEM COME OUT OF A HEAD. YET TO RECOGNIZE THIS FACT DOESN'T MEAN THAT THE AUTHOR'S DESIGN OR INTENTION SHOULD BE USED AS A STANDARD FOR CRITICAL JUDGEMENT.

The implication of Wimsatt and Beardsley's argument was to prioritize the text as the primary **locus of meaning** – rather than the author. This may seem self-limiting and self-referential; however, the New Critics linked the practice of close reading to grand claims about the universal status of a poem's meaning.

The role of the New Critic was to mediate between the particular and the general, between body and spirit, in order to cast light on the universal truths evident in poetry. Poetry is an embodiment of the "concrete universal", giving a specific form to timeless truths.

Russian Formalism

Just before the American New Critics, another formalism developed in the work of a group of Russian literary scholars in the early 20th century.

The group included **Viktor Shklovsky** (1893–1984), **Yury Tynyanov** (1894–1943), **Roman Jakobson** (1896–1982) and **Boris Eichenbaum** (1886–1959), who were influenced by the phenomenology* of **Edmund Husserl** (1859–1938), a German philosopher of science. Husserl's phenomenology was a hermeneutical* method that tried to identify the objects of knowledge as "unmixed essences".

Russian formalism flourished in the years immediately after the Bolshevik revolution in October 1917, but was silenced by the rise of Stalinism in the later 1920s, when so-called "socialist realism" was imposed as cultural policy. This led to a suppression of avant-garde and experimental currents in culture and criticism.

Formalism arose as part of a polemical engagement with symbolist critics, who viewed poetry as an embodiment of spiritual and religious meanings. The Formalists, by contrast, severed this figurative and referential link, looking instead at the mechanics of **textual composition** and **modes of operation** (for example, ways in which Dostoevsky's [1821–81] *Brothers Karamazov* [1880] used devices from the detective novel to subvert prevailing conventions of novelistic realism).

This significantly reduced the importance of the author, anticipating the intentional fallacy argument of the New Critics. The author was viewed less as a creative genius, in the Romantic mould, and more as a manipulator of the various literary conventions and devices. The Formalists were primarily interested in the **internal** functioning of a literary text, rather than the **external** contextual or biographical material that might give rise to a text.

THE OBJECT OF STUDY OF LITERARY SCIENCE IS NOT LITERATURE BUT "LITERARINESS", THAT IS, WHAT MAKES A GIVEN WORK A LITERARY WORK.

The Formalists sought to shift the focus of literary study away from the representational, or mimetic, aspects of literature as a reflection of social reality and set out to determine the specificity of literary language that could be examined as literary language.

Formalist critical vocabulary is often scientific, concerned with art as a device or function for achieving certain effects. Poetic language exists separately from everyday speech insofar as its primary aim is not necessarily to communicate, but operates instead according to its own laws, creating effects through the manipulation of particular devices (e.g. rhythm, repetition, alliteration).

POETRY IS ORGANIZED VIOLENCE COMMITTED ON ORDINARY SPEECH.

One function of literary language, then, is to defamiliarize readers from everyday, habitual patterns of thought by exposing them to the **shock of the new**. Shklovsky elaborated the concept of defamiliarization, or making strange (*ostranenie*), in his essay "Art as Technique" (1917):

THE TECHNIQUE OF ART IS TO MAKE OBJECTS "UNFAMILIAR", TO MAKE FORMS DIFFICULT, TO INCREASE THE DIFFICULTY AND LENGTH OF PERCEPTION ... ART IS A WAY OF EXPERIENCING THE ARTFULNESS OF AN OBJECT; THE OBJECT IS NOT IMPORTANT.

Shklovsky's statement echoes the aestheticism of Pater and Wilde. Other important statements of the Formalists' theory include Eichenbaum's essay "The Theory of the Formal Method" (1926) and the essays

From Literary Criticism to Literary Theory

In the latter half of the 20th century, New Criticism came under pressure. Its methods had proved useful as a teaching tool following the expansion of higher education after WWII, but this expansion was also one factor that led to a political and theoretical turn in literary criticism in the 1960s and 70s. Some of the major theoretical currents of the 20th century can be grouped into overarching movements – such as post-structuralism or New Historicism. But, as you will see, such labels are only partially appropriate.

In this brief introduction, many of these critical methodologies and approaches are treated as discrete groups.

IN PRACTICE, WE NEED TO ACCOUNT FOR THE PATTERNS OF MUTUAL INFLUENCE THAT EXIST BETWEEN THEM.

One of the most salient features of this theoretical turn in literary studies is the emphasis on interdisciplinarity, with its implied critique of narrow specialization. The **interdisciplinary** impetus has encouraged literary critics to engage with other disciplines, including philosophy and anthropology, and has often entailed a radicalization (and politicization) of approach. This returns us to the question of what might constitute the literary critic's proper object of study.

Whereas some people reject theoretical approaches, **Geoffrey Hartman** (b. 1929) has argued that:

IT IS BETTER TO TAKE THE STANDPOINT THAT CRITICISM INFORMED OR MOTIVATED BY THEORY IS PART OF LITERARY CRITICISM (RATHER THAN OF PHILOSOPHY OR AN UNKNOWN SCIENCE) AND THAT LITERARY CRITICISM IS WITHIN LITERATURE, NOT OUTSIDE IT.

In many of the theoretical currents described here, the issue of representation (or mimesis), which can be traced back to classical antiquity in the writings of Plato and Aristotle, reappears as a problem of ideological affinity, group identity and critical self-consciousness.

Structuralism

Structuralism is identified with the work of the Swiss linguist **Ferdinand de Saussure** (1857–1913). His *Course in General Linguistics* (1916) was reconstructed from the lecture notes of his students and published after his death. Saussure's structuralist linguistics entails a set of claims about how language is constructed according to certain rules that are frequently contradicted by particular instances of language use.

SAUSSURE DISTINGUISHED BETWEEN *LANGUE* AND *PAROLE*: THE SYSTEM OF RULES (LANGUE) GOVERNING A LANGUAGE, SUCH AS GRAMMAR AND SYNTAX, VERSUS THE SPECIFIC UTTERANCES (PAROLE) OF INDIVIDUAL LANGUAGE-USERS, WHICH MAKE THESE RULES VISIBLE.

In literal translation, the two terms distinguish between "language" and "speaking", which points to another important division between the written and spoken word.

Saussure broke with the **diachronic** principles underlying previous approaches to the study of language (that is, tracking historical changes in language) and argued instead for a **synchronic** approach: looking at language at a particular point in history. This synchronic approach, according to Saussure, might allow for a thorough, systematic investigation of the relationship between *langue* and *parole* at a given phase in the development of a language.

Saussure viewed language as a system of signs and signifying conventions. Crucially, he argued that the conventions that govern a language are **arbitrary**.

There is no essential connection, for Saussure, between the **"signifier"** (a phonetic construct or sound pattern) and the **"signified"** (mental concept), which, taken together, constitute the linguistic **"sign"**.

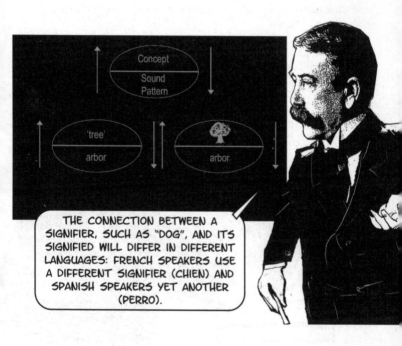

THE CONNECTION BETWEEN A SIGNIFIER, SUCH AS "DOG", AND ITS SIGNIFIED WILL DIFFER IN DIFFERENT LANGUAGES: FRENCH SPEAKERS USE A DIFFERENT SIGNIFIER (CHIEN) AND SPANISH SPEAKERS YET ANOTHER (PERRO).

The relationship between signifier and signified is not entirely random – it is a result of historical development and social convention – but it is arbitrary.

Also important is Saussure's argument that meanings are determined by **difference**: no sign has meaning apart from its differential relationship to other signs. For example, the signifier "cat" signifies the mental concept of a four-legged, furry animal because the signifier cat is not equivalent with the signifiers bat or mat, etc., rather than because the word "cat" contains any essential or inherent dimension of cattiness. As for the signifier "bat", is it a piece of sporting equipment or an animal?

Saussure's linguistics implies a suspension of language's referential function: it presents language as a self-contained system of signs that operates according to certain principles. Meaning is arrived at *negatively*, rather than positively.

Applications of Structuralism

Structuralist linguistics asks us to question whether the world and the things in it can straightforwardly be taken as the referential objects of language.

Saussure instead posited language as an enclosed system in itself. Saussure's linguistics influenced developments in a number of other disciplines, including anthropology, psychoanalysis, philosophy and literary criticism. For example, the anthropologist **Claude Lévi-Strauss** (1908–2009) utilized structuralist methodology in his ethnographic studies of myth and ritual, in which he sought to find the normative patterns or grammar that constitute the structural basis of these cultural phenomena.

I WAS LESS INTERESTED IN THE CONTENT OF ANY PARTICULAR MYTH THAN IN THE STRUCTURE OF RELATIONS BETWEEN ALL MYTHIC NARRATIVES, WHICH MIGHT ENABLE ME TO ARTICULATE THE UNDERLYING RULES GOVERNING THE SYSTEM OF MYTH.

French structuralism took off in the 1950s and 1960s, partly as a development of Russian formalism. The scientific impulse of early formalism was carried over into the structuralist attempt to determine the systematic rules of linguistic and literary phenomena, mapping the underlying (and universal) structures of consciousness that give rise to these phenomena.

For literary criticism, such an approach provided a way of viewing texts as expressions (or symptoms) of a wider system that could be delineated.

This methodology lent itself particularly well to genre criticism, sometimes censured for being overly schematic or inattentive to the particularity of individual works of literature. The confluence of Lévi-Strauss's writings on myth and Vladimir Propp's studies of the folktale (*Morphology of the Folktale*, 1928) helped pioneer the related discipline of narratology.

Later developments in narratology are associated with the work of French literary critic **Roland Barthes** (1915–80), **Tzvetan Todorov** (b. 1939) and **Gérard Genette** (b. 1930). Todorov's "Typology of Detective Fiction", included in *The Poetics of Prose* (1977), exemplifies a genre-based structuralist attempt to classify and explicate the raw "data" of literary material.

THIS WAS A WAY OF BRINGING TO BEAR STRUCTURALIST THOUGHT ON THE READING OF NARRATIVES IN LITERATURE.

Saussure's work opened up a field of possibilities that allowed critics to challenge the (allegedly naive) critical understanding of literary realism.

Rather than assuming that a literary text simply reflects, or mirrors, a given social reality – as was the dominant assumption of traditional criticism concerning the 19th-century realist novel – such texts could also be seen as belonging to a network of **signifying conventions** and **allusive references** to other written works.

IN "THE REALITY EFFECT" (1968), I POINTED TO THE LITTLE DETAILS OF A NARRATIVE – AN OLD PIANO IN A CORNER, OR A HEAP OF UNWASHED CLOTHES – THAT APPEAR SUPERFLUOUS, BUT WHICH MAKE A NARRATIVE SEEM "REAL".

Roland Barthes

Barthes' earlier work, including *Mythologies* (1957) and "Introduction to the Structural Analysis of Narrative" (1966), have an identifiably structuralist emphasis in their analysis of popular culture as a sign-system.

The structuralist suspension of language's referential function was also influential in encouraging some thinkers to examine the inverse: the ways in which social reality itself is constructed through language (sometimes known as the "linguistic turn").

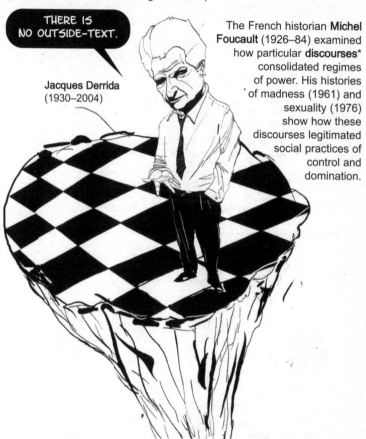

THERE IS NO OUTSIDE-TEXT.

Jacques Derrida (1930–2004)

The French historian **Michel Foucault** (1926–84) examined how particular **discourses*** consolidated regimes of power. His histories of madness (1961) and sexuality (1976) show how these discourses legitimated social practices of control and domination.

The clearest example of Foucault's influence on the study of literature is his essay "What is an Author?" (1969), in which he charts the long-term development of the "**author function**", revealing how the idea of the author – often viewed as timeless or unchanging – varies according to historical context.

From Structuralism to Post-Structuralism

In the late 1960s, some of the main assumptions of structuralist methodology were subjected to a variety of critiques, which have collectively come to be known as post-structuralism.

Many of the thinkers now identified with post-structuralism remained indebted to the insights of Saussure's linguistics, but sought critically to expand its range of possibilities.

The French philosopher Jacques Derrida playfully extended Saussure's concept of linguistic difference, reformulating it as *différance*. Derrida's pun combines the senses "to differ" and "to defer", suggesting not only that meaning is determined negatively through a process of linguistic differentiation, as Saussure had argued, but also that:

MEANING MIGHT BE CEASELESSLY DEFERRED ALONG A SIGNIFYING CHAIN ... COG-DOG-LOG ... WITHOUT ANY POSSIBILITY OF AN ULTIMATE DESTINATION.

dog

cog

log

Derrida's delivery of his essay "Structure, Sign and Play in the Discourse of the Human Sciences" in Baltimore in 1966 is often cited as the moment when post-structuralism first emerged as a challenge to foregoing assumptions of structuralist criticism.

STRUCTURE – OR RATHER THE *STRUCTURALITY* OF STRUCTURE – ALTHOUGH IT HAS ALWAYS BEEN AT WORK, HAS ALWAYS BEEN NEUTRALIZED OR REDUCED BY THE PROCESS OF GIVING IT A CENTRE OR OF REFERRING IT TO A POINT OF PRESENCE, A FIXED POINT OR ORIGIN.

Derrida does not reject the vocabulary of structuralism outright but seeks instead to avoid the neutralization of its radical potential.

Derrida's essay constituted part of a varied critique of the ruling logocentrism of the Western philosophical tradition. **Logocentrism** takes its name from *Logos* (the Word of God) and refers to a hermeneutic tradition based on the search for absolute meaning, authority, origin and teleology, grounded in the assumption that language and reality are transparent to one another – that nothing gets "lost in translation" when moving between words and the reality they are taken to represent. Such assumptions tended to ignore the way in which linguistic meaning can slip and slide away from itself.

Derrida's critique of logocentrism, by contrast, is often seen as a celebration of indeterminacy, interpretative play and multiplicity. His *Of Grammatology* (1967) offers a sustained interrogation, or **"deconstruction"**, of the work of Saussure and Lévi-Strauss, and *Writing and Difference* (1967) contains essays on Hegel, Freud and Foucault.

Roland Barthes' essay "The Death of the Author" (1968) marked his own break with structuralism, culminating in a radical challenge to traditional accounts of human subjectivity. In this essay, Barthes argued that:

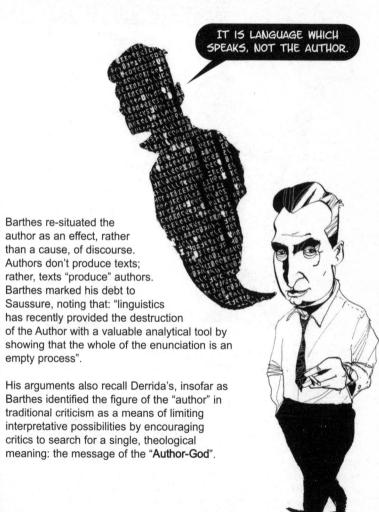

IT IS LANGUAGE WHICH SPEAKS, NOT THE AUTHOR.

Barthes re-situated the author as an effect, rather than a cause, of discourse. Authors don't produce texts; rather, texts "produce" authors. Barthes marked his debt to Saussure, noting that: "linguistics has recently provided the destruction of the Author with a valuable analytical tool by showing that the whole of the enunciation is an empty process".

His arguments also recall Derrida's, insofar as Barthes identified the figure of the "author" in traditional criticism as a means of limiting interpretative possibilities by encouraging critics to search for a single, theological meaning: the message of the "**Author-God**".

WE KNOW THAT TO GIVE WRITING ITS FUTURE, IT IS NECESSARY TO OVERTHROW THE MYTH: THE BIRTH OF THE READER MUST BE AT THE COST OF THE DEATH OF THE AUTHOR.

Barthes was interested in "liberating" the text from the straightjacket of traditionalist criticism, allowing for a proliferation of interpretative possibilities.

Other thinkers identified with the displacement of structuralism included **Julia Kristeva** (b. 1941), **Luce Irigaray** (b. 1930), **Jean-François Lyotard** (1924–98) and **Jean Baudrillard** (1929–2007). This intellectual current is notable for its iconoclastic interrogation of "grand narratives", such as humanism and Marxism. Lyotard's *The Post-Modern Condition* (1979) set out to demolish the claims of these metanarratives and their claims of universality. He saw Enlightenment rationalism as coercive – along with the political and philosophical traditions that stemmed from it.

Marxist Literary Theory

Marxist theory and practice is, first and foremost, a strategic orientation and critical methodology, which aims to transform collective social life. Marxists aspire towards the supersession of the capitalist mode of production. Unlike liberal and conservative thinkers, who tend to regard capitalism as the best of all possible worlds, despite its many injustices and inequalities, thinkers influenced by **Karl Marx** (1818–83) and by the wider socialist tradition regard capitalism as an unstable phase in the continuing development of human history.

Marxists investigate ways in which the economic organization of capitalist society, oriented around competition and exploitation, produces social and class antagonisms. This state of affairs leads to struggle between classes, but these struggles have no pre-determined outcome, hence the importance of human agency and intervention.

Marx's historical view of capitalist society has often led Marxist critics of literature and culture to be particularly sensitive to the historicity (historical authenticity or actuality) of literary forms and genres. No one writes like Homer anymore and this has as much, if not more, to do with historical changes in social and economic structure as it does with the individual whims of particular authors.

Homer's epics, for example, presupposed the mythic narratives that belonged to the cultural atmosphere of classical Greece, but that felt out of place in the mid-19th century:

WHAT CHANCE HAS VULCAN AGAINST ROBERTS AND CO., JUPITER AGAINST THE LIGHTNING-ROD AND HERMES AGAINST THE CREDIT MOBILIER?

If literary texts in some sense *reflect* their material, historical and social conditions of production, then claims about the capacity of literature to depict timeless truths of the human condition begin to look shaky, not least because the "human condition" itself is, for Marxists, another historical construction.

The writings of Marx and **Friedrich Engels** (1820–95) were primarily concerned with economics, politics and philosophy. They made only fragmentary comments on art and literature and didn't elaborate a systematic aesthetic theory. As such, Marxist criticism of literature has been developed by a wide range of writers influenced by, but not beholden to, Marx's ideas.

Marx's thought was self-consciously oppositional, not least because "the ruling ideas of each age have ever been the ideas of its ruling class", as he quipped in *The Communist Manifesto*. Accordingly, Marxist critics have focused on issues including the role of literature as a form of ideological reproduction in capitalist society as well as the status of literary works as **cultural commodities**.

For much of the 20th century, Marxist criticism was identified with the "vulgar", Soviet style of literary criticism, which reduced the role of criticism to an ideological analysis of the content of literary works, subordinating aesthetics to politics.

After the defeat of the Bolshevik revolution in the 1920s, the theory and practice of so-called socialist realism became cultural policy, requiring Soviet artists and writers to produce edifying representations of the construction of socialism in the USSR.

Leon Trotsky (1879–1940) had articulated a less domineering perspective in *Literature and Revolution* (1924):

A WORK OF ART SHOULD, IN THE FIRST PLACE, BE JUDGED BY ITS OWN LAW, THAT IS, BY THE LAW OF ART.

MARXISM ALONE CAN EXPLAIN WHY AND HOW A GIVEN TENDENCY IN ART HAS ORIGINATED IN A GIVEN PERIOD OF HISTORY.

Trotsky also criticized the Russian Formalist School for its "abortive idealism":

THEY BELIEVE THAT "IN THE BEGINNING WAS THE WORD". BUT WE BELIEVE THAT IN THE BEGINNING WAS THE DEED.

One notable feature of socialist realism was its hostility to all forms of artistic modernism and aesthetic experimentation. Much of the literary criticism of the Hungarian Marxist **Georg Lukács** (1885–1971) was devoted to polemical attacks on modernism because of its perceived subjectivism.

Lukács had offered a particularly sensitive appreciation of the novel in his pre-Marxist work *The Theory of the Novel* (1920). Much of his later work also concerned the novel. His critical studies of contemporary writers, particularly the German novelist **Thomas Mann** (1875–1955), were guided by an attempt to make 19th-century realism viable as a model of literary creation and social critique in the crisis-ridden conditions of the mid-20th century.

Realism was Lukács's preferred genre. His defence of realism is linked to his concepts of reflection and typicality. Realist literature, for Lukács, provides a reflection of the complex totality of social life with characters who typify world-historical conditions.

His study of the 19th-century novel was characterized by a sympathetic engagement with the critical insights of the bourgeois cultural heritage. He developed these ideas in books including *The Historical Novel* (1947) and *Studies in European Realism* (1950). In these works, Lukács was partly indebted to Engels' fragmentary comments on realism as a genre in an 1888 letter to the minor English novelist **Margaret Harkness** (1854–1923):

REALISM, TO MY MIND, IMPLIES, BESIDES TRUTH OF DETAIL, THE TRUTHFUL REPRODUCTION OF TYPICAL CHARACTERS UNDER TYPICAL CIRCUMSTANCES.

In the 1930s, Lukács debated the nature of realism with a number of other German Marxist critics, including Walter Benjamin, **Ernst Bloch** (1885–1977) and Theodor Adorno. Benjamin's writings on Brecht's drama were a high-point in mid-20th-century Marxist cultural criticism, as was his essay on the effects of mechanical reproducibility on the "aura" of a work of art.

Benjamin was loosely affiliated to the Frankfurt School, known for major figures including Adorno, **Max Horkheimer** (1895–1973) and **Herbert Marcuse** (1898–1979), who drew on the work of Marx and Freud in elaborating a critical theory of late-capitalist society. During the Nazi dictatorship, the Frankfurt School emigrated to the USA, where its leading thinkers continued to develop their critique of the "culture industry" and the homogenizing effects of mass culture. This group of writers is sometimes referred to under the label of Western (i.e. non-Soviet) Marxism.

In *Marxism and Form* (1971), the American Marxist critic **Fredric Jameson** (b. 1934) introduced the work of major thinkers in the Western Marxist tradition into anglophone intellectual culture. Jameson drew upon the work of six European Marxists – Adorno, Benjamin, Marcuse, Bloch, Lukács and Sartre – to formulate a dialectical* theory of literary history.

THE THINKER'S AWARENESS OF HIS POSITION IN SOCIETY AND HISTORY CONTENDS WITH THE LIMITS IMPOSED ON THIS AWARENESS BY HIS CLASS POSITION.

In his more recent work, Jameson has focused on postmodernism as the cultural logic of late capitalist society and the expressions of a utopian impulse in modern culture. Jameson has elsewhere reiterated his commitment to historicism.

ALWAYS HISTORICIZE!

The British Marxist critic **Terry Eagleton** (b. 1943) in his introduction to *Marxism and Literary Criticism* (1976) reminded readers that:

> MARXIST CRITICISM IS NOT JUST AN ALTERNATIVE TECHNIQUE FOR INTERPRETING *PARADISE LOST* OR *MIDDLEMARCH*. IT IS PART OF OUR LIBERATION FROM OPPRESSION.

> THE PRIMARY TASK OF THE "MARXIST CRITIC" IS TO ACTIVELY PARTICIPATE IN AND HELP DIRECT THE CULTURAL EMANCIPATION OF THE MASSES.

Be Realistic: Demand the Impossible

This overtly political stance is a characteristic aspect of Marxist criticism. Eagleton would also readily acknowledge his debt to the work of **Raymond Williams** (1921–88). Central to both Williams's and Eagleton's critical work has been a refusal of the reductive view that sees a deterministic (or causal) relationship between economic "base" and cultural "superstructure". This view risks seeing cultural production as a simplistic reflection of economic forces and overlooks its dynamic role in ideological production.

Psychoanalysis

The work of **Sigmund Freud** (1856–1939) laid the foundations of psychoanalysis as a method of treating mental disorders that encourages patients to confront repressed fears and anxieties often manifest in the interaction between conscious and unconscious elements of the mind. It is frequently associated with the so-called talking cure.

Freud's "discovery" of the unconscious – especially his elaboration of its working through the interpretation of dreams – had important implications for our understanding of human consciousness and subjectivity. Freudian psychoanalysis implies a host of hidden or "repressed" motivations for human behaviour that undermine the unity and coherence of the bourgeois subject.

Some have noted a parallel between psychoanalytic accounts of human subjectivity and the Marxist critique of class society, insofar as "repression" plays an important role in both theories.

Freud's psychoanalytic writings often take the form of case studies, analysing the neurotic behaviour of particular individuals. He also used literary texts as a source for psychoanalytic interpretation. For instance, Freud's essay "Das Unheimliche", translated into English as "The Uncanny" in 1919, is organized around a reading of **E.T.A. Hoffman**'s (1776–1822) short story "The Sandman" (1816). In the essay, he interprets the fear of losing one's eyes – a running motif in Hoffman's story – as a symbolic manifestation of the fear of castration, bound up with Oedipal guilt.

Freud also made use of literary examples in formulating his theories of human subjectivity, famously drawing on the narrative of Oedipus – familiar from classical mythology and Sophocles' *Oedipus Rex* – in elaborating the Oedipus complex, which was central to his view of the human condition.

Freud defined the basic elements of what he would later characterize as a "complex" in a letter to **Wilhelm Fliess** (1858–1928), with a startling self-analysis:

I TOO HAVE FALLEN IN LOVE WITH MY MOTHER AND FELT JEALOUS OF MY FATHER, AND I NOW REGARD IT AS A UNIVERSAL EVENT OF EARLY CHILDHOOD.

He also speculated whether the Oedipus complex might help explain Shakespeare's *Hamlet*. According to Freud, Hamlet's hesitation in killing his uncle Claudius (who murdered Hamlet's father) stems from Hamlet's own unconscious awareness that he harboured the same desires as Claudius, i.e. to kill his father and possess his mother.

Literary texts continued to provide a source of theoretical insight for later key psychoanalytic figures, developing Freud's work in new directions. For instance, the French psychoanalyst **Jacques Lacan** (1901–81) examined "The Purloined Letter" (1844) – a short detective story by the American writer **Edgar Allan Poe** (1809–49) – in two lectures: "Seminar on 'The Purloined Letter'" (1956) and "The Instance of the Letter in the Unconscious, or Reason Since Freud" (1957). Influenced by structuralist linguistics, Lacan suggested that manifestations of the unconscious (such as dreams or neurotic symptoms) could be interpreted *as if they were texts*.

THE UNCONSCIOUS IS STRUCTURED LIKE A LANGUAGE.

Many point to the way in which psychoanalytic clinical practice – which revolves around the relationship between patient and analyst – structurally mirrors the practices of literary interpretation in which the critic (or analyst) teases out latent meanings from the literary text's (or patient's) manifest content.

More broadly, psychoanalysis offers a way of thinking about human subjectivity that disturbs the notion of a centred, rational, thinking subject for whom thought is a transparent medium. Freud's "discovery" of the unconscious fundamentally undermined the influential axiom of Cartesian subjectivity (*I think, therefore I am*), breaking the link between thought and being, or between the interior world of the subject and the external world of appearances and actions.

This has prompted literary critics to reconsider ways of approaching the problem of **authorial intention**. If an intention is assumed to be unconsciously present, rather than stated, this assumption will require a hermeneutical approach that treats statements as *symptomatic* rather than expressive utterances, and that does not naively assume a transparent relationship between author and text, or between statement and intention.

Questions of narrative perspective in a realist novel, or of strategies of self-representation in a lyric poem, appear in a different light if we can no longer safely assume that human consciousness is straightforwardly knowable.

The insights of psychoanalytic theory have informed the work of a wide range of 20th-century literary critics. In an essay that first appeared in 1977 in a special issue of *Yale French Studies* devoted to literature and psychoanalysis, **Shoshana Felman** (b. 1942) re-reads **Henry James**' *The Turn of the Screw* (1898) – ostensibly a ghost story – as a psychological case study in neurosis, locating moments of linguistic ambiguity that point towards interpretative possibilities within the text.

Felman built on Edmund Wilson's argument in "The Ambiguity of Henry James" (1938) that James' narrative actually depicts a neurosis resulting from sexual repression of the narrative's protagonist, a young governess.

I EXPLORED WHETHER THE AMBIGUITY IDENTIFIED BY WILSON MIGHT, IN FACT, BE FUNDAMENTAL TO THE PROCESS OF *ALL* LITERARY INTERPRETATION.

The insights of psychoanalysis could help reveal the way in which such ambiguities are deeply embedded in human consciousness.

Some Versions of Historicism

Historicism, or the historical view of literature, can be traced back the work of the 18th-century Italian philosopher **Giambattista Vico** (1668–1774) and the German philosopher and poet **Johann Gottfried von Herder** (1744–1803). Their historicism influenced later thinkers, including **G.W.F. Hegel** (1770–1831) and Karl Marx. The historical view of the work of classical writers and theorists questioned the universal basis of appreciation, across all times and places, focusing instead on the specificity of context and historical period (a kind of relativism*).

This historical way of thinking – which can be identified with the claim that knowledge itself is historically conditioned – was influential for much of the 18th and 19th centuries.

In the 1980s, the American literary critic **Stephen Greenblatt** (b. 1943) coined the term "New Historicism" to describe his own research on Elizabethan drama. The phrase first appeared in his introduction to a collection of essays he edited, *The Power of Forms in the English Renaissance* (1982). The majority of New Historicist criticism focuses on the Renaissance.

New Historicism can be understood as a partial return to a historical way of reading literature, in the wake of New Criticism's formalist emphasis on the specificity of the literary text and the "words on the page", which has often been accused of being a-historical.

EYES ON THE PAGE!

BUT THERE'S SO MUCH ELSE GOING ON HERE!

The dominant historicist trend in literary studies (which had been displaced by New Criticism), saw the critic's function as an attempt to elucidate the connections between literary texts and their historical, biographical, social and cultural context. *New* Historicism inaugurated a "return" to the historical archive. This return, however, was mediated by the theoretical advances of structuralism and post-structuralism, particularly the work of Michel Foucault, whose studies in the history of discourses such as madness and sexuality offered a new, theoretically-informed way of navigating the vast swathes of archival material.

WE NEED TO GO BACK IN TIME TO GET THE MOST FROM THIS TEXT.

A New Historicist critic influenced by Foucault's historical writing might trace patterns of *discourse* through an array of texts, selected not so much for their "literary" content, as for the way in which **textuality*** itself reveals the circulation of particular, historically determined discourses.

Tracing the circulation of a particular discourse can, in turn, reveal the **structures of power** that operate in a given social environment, as well as the ways in which certain kinds of textual and cultural practice might be mobilized to subvert such power-structures.

WE ALSO STRENUOUSLY AVOIDED IMPOSING ANY "GRAND NARRATIVE" ON THESE TEXTUALLY-MEDIATED HISTORICAL EVENTS.

One result of New Historicism has been to broaden the range and type of material that the literary critic might regard as a "legitimate" area of study, thus collapsing some of the previously accepted hierarchies between the "literary" and "non-literary" that had motivated previous critical practices.

Literary criticism begins to veer off, at this point, into cultural and intellectual history. Discourses of power might be just as visible in an obscure polemical tract or "minor" broadside ballad as in a "major" Shakespearean tragedy.

New Historicism and Cultural Materialism

Greenblatt's writings on Renaissance drama in *Renaissance Self-Fashioning: From More to Shakespeare* (1980) diverge and converge with the work of **Alan Sinfield** (b. 1941) and **Jonathan Dollimore** (b. 1948), whose edited collection of essays *Political Shakespeare: Essays in Cultural Materialism* (1985) includes Greenblatt's "Invisible Bullets". The collection also points to ways in which Shakespeare's plays could be understood with reference to the discourses and practices of colonialism and patriarchy. In the foreword, Sinfield and Dollimore define their aim:

CULTURAL MATERIALISM DOES NOT, LIKE MUCH ESTABLISHED LITERARY CRITICISM, ATTEMPT TO MYSTIFY ITS PERSPECTIVE AS THE NATURAL, OBVIOUS OR RIGHT INTERPRETATION OF AN ALLEGEDLY GIVEN TEXTUAL FACT.

ON THE CONTRARY, IT REGISTERS ITS COMMITMENT TO THE TRANSFORMATION OF A SOCIAL ORDER WHICH EXPLOITS PEOPLE ON GROUNDS OF RACE, GENDER AND CLASS.

Cultural materialism, which also emerged in the 1980s, is not entirely synonymous with New Historicism. Some cultural materialists were sceptical of the Foucauldian motivations of New Historicism: to them, networks of power do not only operate at the level of discourse, but also have specific material, social and economic determinations. New Historicists tended to disregard these as a result of their focus on textuality.

The reassertion of a **materialist historicism** originated within a Marxist milieu. It is identified most closely with **Raymond Williams** (1921–88), who, in books such as *Marxism and Literature* (1977) and *Problems in Materialism and Culture* (1980), attempted to extend a materialist method of social analysis into the realm of cultural production.

Williams's work ranged across diverse forms of 20th-century cultural production and mass communication, including film and television. His writings were also influential in pioneering the discipline of cultural studies, which carved out a prominent niche at the University of Birmingham between 1964 and 2002, under the direction of **Richard Hoggart** (1918–2014) and, later, **Stuart Hall** (1932–2014).

The work originating within the Birmingham Centre for Contemporary **Cultural Studies** problematized the traditional distinction between "high" and "low" culture and scrutinized the effects of **mass culture**, with a particular focus on class and education.

Feminism

"Second-wave" feminist criticism emerged and flourished in tandem with the social movements of the 1960s. This critical movement focused attention on the representation of women's experience in literature, particularly the novel.

Many second-wave feminists also sought to reengage and reinterpret the critical legacy of "first-wave" feminism, which is strongly identified with (but not reducible to) the 19th- and early-20th-century struggle for women's suffrage.

The ideological origins of feminism and the struggle for women's liberation are often traced back to **Mary Wollstonecraft**'s (1759–97) *A Vindication of the Rights of Woman* (1792) and **John Stuart Mill**'s (1806–73) *The Subjection of Women* (1869).

The influence of second-wave feminism within literary criticism was most pronounced in two areas:

1. Questioning and exposing the **phallocentric** (male-dominated) **bias** in mainstream culture
2. The critical recovery of overlooked female writers and the overlooked tradition of women's writing.

Kate Millett's (b.1934) *Sexual Politics* (1969) and **Elaine Showalter**'s (b.1941) *A Literature of Their Own: British Women Novelists from Brontë to Lessing* (1977) were influential in anglophone criticism in both confronting patriarchy and elucidating the existence of an alternative tradition of women's writing. Millett offers a strident critique of the misogynistic sexual politics of four 20th-century male writers: D.H. Lawrence (1885–1930), Henry Miller (1891–1980), Norman Mailer (1923–2007) and Jean Genet (1910–86).

MAILER'S WORK DISPLAYS A REACTIONARY SEXUAL ATTITUDE THAT ERUPTS INTO OPEN HOSTILITY.

Developments in French feminism had been influenced by the publication of **Simone de Beauvoir**'s (1908–86) *The Second Sex* (1949). This landmark book questioned the social construction and representation of gender roles.

Later departures formed part of the atmosphere of revolutionary upheaval sparked by the events of 1968 and the post-structuralist concerns with a transformed conception of human subjectivity and signifying practices.

Hélène Cixous (b. 1937) coined the term *écriture féminine* (literally translated as "feminine writing") in *The Laugh of Medusa* (1976) to refer to a kind of writing unmarked by the traces of phallogocentric discourse. **Phallogocentrism** was seen as the product of logocentrism and phallocentrism (where the phallus stands in for male power and domination in a patriarchal society).

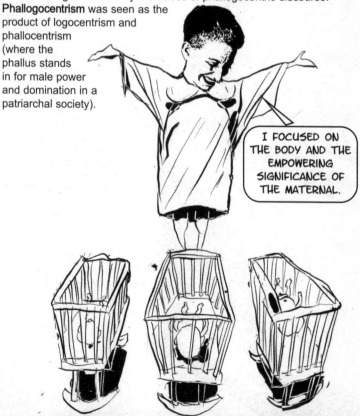

I FOCUSED ON THE BODY AND THE EMPOWERING SIGNIFICANCE OF THE MATERNAL.

Other feminists, including **Monique Wittig** (1935–2003), challenged this focus on the body as biologically reductive and argued that the idea of *écriture feminine* was guilty of an essentializing universalism. **Essentialism** here refers to a focus on the social and psychological factors that constitute female experience and that are assumed to be common to all women.

ESSENTIALISM CREATES THE UNIVERSAL SUBJECT OF FEMINIST STRUGGLE AS DEFINED AGAINST MALE EXPERIENCE AND THOUGHT.

THE LABEL OF "WOMEN'S WRITER" IS OVERLY RESTRICTIVE. I REJECT IT, AND INSTEAD DESCRIBE MYSELF AS A "RADICAL LESBIAN".

Relativists, by contrast, question the implied universality of the "category" of womanhood.

138

Partly as a result of these debates, contemporary feminism is hardly unified in approach. In the 1960s and 70s, one of the key debates among second-wave feminists concerned the possibility of an *essential difference* between writing by women and writing by men, expressing fundamental disparities between male and female experience.

Showalter formulated the concept of "**gynocriticism**":

THE PROGRAMME OF GYNOCRITICS IS TO CONSTRUCT A FEMALE FRAMEWORK FOR THE ANALYSIS OF WOMEN'S LITERATURE, TO DEVELOP NEW MODELS BASED ON THE STUDY OF FEMALE EXPERIENCE.

Toril Moi (b. 1953), in *Sexual/Textual Politics* (1985) responded to Showalter from a post-structuralist background, accusing her of essentialism.

WHAT FEMINISTS SUCH AS SHOWALTER FAIL TO GRASP IS THAT THE TRADITIONAL HUMANISM THEY REPRESENT IS PART OF PATRIARCHAL IDEOLOGY.

Intersectionality

Much feminist criticism has operated at an intersection with other theoretical traditions, including psychoanalysis and Marxism. The intersection of gender, race, class and sexual identities also led some feminists to question essentialist, undifferentiated constructions of the category of womanhood, pointing to the many differences (of race and class) that make it problematic to think about the notion of female experience as shared by all women.

INTERSECTIONALITY REFERS TO THE STUDY OF LINKS BETWEEN DIFFERENT KINDS OF OPPRESSION AND DOMINATION.

The self-described "lesbian, mother, warrior, poet" **Audre Lorde** (1934–92) criticized a perceived white bias within second-wave feminism. In her essay "The Master's Tools Will Never Dismantle the Master's House" (1984) she argued that feminist attempts to achieve reforms of the dominant patriarchal system can lead some white feminists unconsciously to adopt elements of the oppressive logic of the ruling system, assuming a universalizing subjectivity, predominantly identified as white and heterosexual.

Gender Studies

Second-wave feminist criticism precipitated close examination of the category of gender. Gender studies is wider in scope than feminism, as it also includes gay and lesbian criticism, as well as **queer theory**.

The major concerns of gender studies are:

1. To examine the political histories of oppression suffered by groups that fall outside the **heteronormative*** paradigm
2. To examine the social construction and representation of gender roles, in which literature plays an important part.

Much of the critical impetus of gender studies derived from real social struggles. The 1969 Stonewall Riots in New York, for example, were a key moment in the history of the gay liberation movement.

The biological distinction between the "male" and "female" sex cannot be neatly mapped onto the gender categories of "masculine" (= male) and "feminine" (= female) because the behavioural traits associated with these categories do not exist as a **binary opposition**.

We might instead think of a spectrum of masculine-identified and feminine-identified behaviours distributed unevenly between men and women. The process of such identification is socially and historically determined. At the biological level, too, the binary logic is destabilized by transsexuality.

GENDER ISN'T AS STRAIGHTFORWARD AS MAINSTREAM CULTURE TENDS TO PORTRAY IT; THERE'S A GREY AREA OF GENDER IDENTIFICATION. THIS IS WHAT WE MEAN WHEN WE TALK ABOUT GENDER BEING "NON-BINARY".

The theorization of gender created a difficulty for feminism because if gender is understood to be an unstable and constructed category then who can be said to constitute the subject of *fem*inism?

Critical insights about gender, which emerged within feminist theory, took on a distinct and separate character (gender studies) as lesbian critics began to challenge the alleged "heteronormative essentialism" of some feminist thinkers. This saw the emergence of a radical strand of feminism: lesbian separatism, which asserted complete female independence and a refusal of masculinist exploitation.

Sexuality, and the politics of sexuality, opened up a field of interpretative possibilities partly distinct from, although still related to, feminism.

OUR CATEGORIES ARE IMPORTANT. WE CANNOT ORGANIZE A SOCIAL LIFE, A POLITICAL MOVEMENT OR OUR INDIVIDUAL IDENTITIES AND DESIRES WITHOUT THEM.

Gayle Rubin
(b. 1949)

Key Figures in the Development of Gay and Lesbian Studies

Guy Hocquengham (1946–88) theorized the psychological impetuses of homophobia.

Jeffrey Weeks (b. 1945), a historian and sociologist, has written widely on gender behaviour, the sphere of the intimate, and gay and lesbian sexuality.

Bonnie Zimmerman (b. 1947) has scrutinized essentialist constructions of female identity, highlighting differences of race, class and particularly sexuality. Some of these arguments are elaborated in her essay "What Has Never Been: An Overview of Lesbian Feminist Literary Criticism" (1981).

Adrienne Rich (1929–2012), an American poet, expressed a lesbian separatism that tended towards dissociation from allegiances with the male gay community.

145

Homosexual Identity and Critical Re-Readings

The articulation of different forms of homosexual identity can be traced back to historical moments in which the public expression of gay or lesbian identity was socially (and legally) proscribed and thus rendered "invisible".

From the 1970s onwards, the new theoretical self-consciousness about sexuality and gender created wide scope for critical re-reading of the work of earlier thinkers and writers whose sexuality had previously been ignored, passed over in silence, or made the object of spectacular public prosecution. For example, *The Well of Loneliness*, by **Radclyffe Hall** (1880–1943), an important early 20th-century lesbian novel, was at the centre of intense legal battles when it first appeared in 1928.

The fin de siècle also proved to be a particularly rich seam in this regard, particularly the work of **Walt Whitman** (1819–92), **Edward Carpenter** (1844–1929), Walter Pater and Oscar Wilde (who was prosecuted and imprisoned for his sexuality in 1895).

FOR US, IT IS HARD TO REGARD WILDE AS OTHER THAN THE APOGEE OF GAY EXPERIENCE AND EXPRESSION, BECAUSE THAT IS THE POSITION WE HAVE ACCORDED HIM IN OUR CULTURES. FOR US, HE IS ALWAYS – ALREADY QUEER – AS THAT STEREOTYPE HAS PREVAILED IN THE 20TH CENTURY.

Some of the most widely-known critical work on gender and sexuality within literary studies is the writing of **Eve Kosofsky Sedgwick** (1950–2009) and **Judith Butler** (b. 1956). Sedgwick questioned the heteronormative bias in mainstream culture and the way in which this (often unconscious) bias has affected the reading of literature. She studied the patterns of homosociality and male homosexual panic in the 19th-century novel and the "paranoid Gothic" genre in *Between Men: English Literature and Male Homosocial Desire* (1985) and *Epistemology of the Closet* (1990).

HOMOSOCIALITY REFERS TO SAME-SEX RELATIONSHIPS OF A NON-SEXUAL NATURE (I.E. FRIENDSHIP OR MENTORSHIP). SEDGWICK POINTED TO WAYS IN WHICH MALE HOMOSOCIALITY IS OFTEN INTERRUPTED BY HOMOSEXUAL PANIC.

THE EASY ASSUMPTION THAT SEXUALITY AND HETEROSEXUALITY ARE ALWAYS EXACTLY TRANSLATABLE INTO ANOTHER IS, OBVIOUSLY, HOMOPHOBIC.

Butler's work can be seen as the height of the social constructionist view of gender theory. Her book *Gender Trouble: Feminism and the Subversion of Identity* (1990) examines gender as a social and cultural performance, rather than an inherent aspect of human nature.

By critically engaging with the work of previous feminist thinkers, such as Simone de Beauvoir, Butler extended the critique of essentialist constructions of female identity, problematizing the identity of "woman". *Bodies that Matter: On the Discursive Limits of Sex* (1993) furthered her thinking on the way gender is constituted by performative acts.

Butler's work offers a critique of stable identity categories (such as "woman" or "queer") as a basis for emancipatory politics.

AS MUCH AS IT IS NECESSARY TO ASSERT POLITICAL DEMANDS THROUGH RECOURSE TO IDENTITY CATEGORIES, AND TO LAY CLAIM TO THE POWER TO NAME ONESELF AND DETERMINE THE CONDITIONS UNDER WHICH THAT NAME IS USED, IT IS ALSO IMPOSSIBLE TO SUSTAIN THAT KIND OF MASTERY OVER THE TRAJECTORY OF THOSE CATEGORIES WITHIN DISCOURSE.

By asserting the performative potential of gender, Butler suggests a way in which multiple non-essentialist understandings of gender roles might enable tentative coalitions to emerge, outside of the constrictive frameworks of masculinist domination and compulsory heterosexuality.

Postcolonial Studies

Postcolonial criticism offers a political approach to literary criticism. It arose in a historical context of decolonization and national liberation struggles in the so-called "third world" in the latter half of the 20th century after the end of WWII. Some of the writers most closely identified with postcolonial criticism participated in these struggles.

Frantz Fanon (1925–61) was born in Martinique, which was a French colony at the time (and which remains an overseas department of France). Fanon participated in the Algerian War of Independence (1954–62) against the French state and offered a Marxist account of the conditions of anti-colonial revolution in *The Wretched of the Earth* (1961).

Fanon, who was also a psychiatrist, wrote a polemical critique of the psychology of colonial domination in *Black Skin, White Masks* (1952). It was as much a study of the formation of black identity under imperialist oppression as it was a critique of the imperialist world order. Fanon characterized the formation of black identity under colonial conditions as a process of "self-division":

> EVERY COLONIZED PEOPLE – IN OTHER WORDS, EVERY PEOPLE IN WHOSE SOUL AN INFERIORITY COMPLEX HAS BEEN CREATED BY THE DEATH AND BURIAL OF ITS LOCAL CULTURAL ORIGINALITY – FINDS ITSELF FACE TO FACE WITH THE LANGUAGE OF THE CIVILIZING NATION; THAT IS, WITH THE CULTURE OF THE MOTHER COUNTRY.

Can the Master's Tools Dismantle the Master's House?

This situation presents a political and strategic problem for colonial peoples about whether to appropriate the culture of the mother country or to reject it entirely in order to assert political, cultural and national autonomy.

Fanon was initially influenced by the writing of **Aimé Césaire** (1913–2008), a founder of the **negritude** movement: a separatist celebration of black culture in francophone literature. Césaire had taught Fanon in Martinique, and his *Discourse on Colonialism* (1950) examines the antagonism between colonizers and colonized.

The colonial project justifies itself as a "civilizing mission", but its motivations were not at all generous or high-minded. Rather, the colonial project was about economic exploitation, backed up with frequent violence.

IT IS EQUALLY NECESSARY TO DECOLONIZE OUR MINDS, OUR INNER LIFE, AT THE SAME TIME THAT WE DECOLONIZE SOCIETY.

Colonial domination mirrors the relationship between the bourgeois and proletariat in classical Marxist theory. Postcolonial criticism derives partly from the Marxist critique of imperialism and colonialism, although not all postcolonial critics would choose to identify as Marxists.

That this economic relationship between metropole and colony also had a cultural dimension was one of the factors that led to the Havana Tricontinental conference of 1966 and subsequent journal *Tricontinental*, which aimed to ally the peoples of Africa, Asia and Latin America against imperialism and to develop the political element of postcolonial studies.

In 1989, **Bill Ashcroft** (b. 1946), **Gareth Griffiths** (b. 1943) and **Helen Tiffin** (b. 1945) collaborated to produce *The Empire Writes Back*, which theorized the importance of postcolonialism for the study of literature, concentrating particularly on the work of **Lewis Nkosi** (1936–2010), **V.S. Naipaul** (b. 1932), **Michael Anthony** (b. 1930), **Timothy Findley** (1930–2002), **Janet Frame** (1924–2004) and **R.K. Narayan** (1906–2001).

WE USE THE TERM "POSTCOLONIAL" TO COVER ALL THE CULTURE AFFECTED BY THE IMPERIAL PROCESS, FROM THE MOMENT OF COLONIZATION TO THE PRESENT DAY.

The importance of the literary canon in perpetuating a form of Western cultural imperialism was challenged by the Kenyan writer **Ngugi Wa Thiong'o** (b. 1938) in his essay "On the Abolition of the English Department" (1968).

The critical contribution of postcolonial studies falls broadly into three main areas:

1. The critique of Eurocentrism
2. The critique of nationalism (even its anti-colonial varieties)
3. The theorization of the subaltern* or subalternity (see page 160).

We can think about these three ideas with reference to the work of the Palestinian-American scholar **Edward Said** (1935–2003) and the Indian-born critics **Homi K. Bhaba** (b. 1949) and **Gayatri Chakravorty Spivak** (b. 1942), all of whom have had a wide-reaching influence within literary studies.

Such approaches have helped further critical understanding of the cultural, political and economic legacies of colonialism and de-colonization.

Orientalism

Said's *Orientalism* (1978),
as well as his later work,
including *Culture and
Imperialism* (1993),
critiqued homogenizing
representations that
construct the East, or
"the Orient", according
to particular discursive
prejudices and
stereotypes.

ORIENTALISM CAN BE DISCUSSED
AND ANALYZED AS THE CORPORATE
INSTITUTION FOR DEALING WITH THE
ORIENT – DEALING WITH IT BY MAKING
STATEMENTS ABOUT IT, AUTHORIZING
VIEWS OF IT, DESCRIBING IT, BY
TEACHING IT, SETTLING IT, RULING
OVER IT: IN SHORT, ORIENTALISM AS
A WESTERN STYLE FOR DOMINATING,
RESTRUCTURING AND HAVING
AUTHORITY OVER THE ORIENT.

As Said showed, many canonical writers of the so-called Western tradition, from Alexander Pope to **Gustave Flaubert** (1821–80), played a part in this process of systematic misrepresentation.

ORIENTALISM ALSO REFERS TO THE WAY IN WHICH EUROPEAN CULTURE HAS MANAGED AND PRODUCED THE IDEA OF THE ORIENT.

The critique of Orientalism belonged to a wider project: an attempt to "unthink Eurocentrism" by laying bare its ugly discursive history in Western culture. Partly influenced by Foucault, Said's range of reference was not exclusively "literary". He was also a committed public intellectual in (critical) solidarity with the Palestinian national liberation movement.

Homi K. Bhaba's writing on the idea of the nation builds upon **Benedict Anderson**'s (b. 1936) theorization of the nation as an "imagined community". The nation is always in the process of being made and re-made in discourse.

Bhaba is particularly critical of the way in which nationalist movements attempt to impose and institutionalize a "unisonant" narrative of the nation (that is, in which all citizens sing from the same hymn sheet), stifling its real multiplicity and diversity. His focus on the concept of "hybridity" is particularly important in expressing the fluid constitution of national identity.

AMERICA LEADS TO AFRICA; THE NATIONS OF EUROPE AND ASIA MEET IN AUSTRALIA; THE MARGINS OF THE NATION DISPLACE THE CENTRE; THE PEOPLES OF THE PERIPHERY RETURN TO REWRITE THE HISTORY AND FICTION OF THE METROPOLIS.

Spivak's essay "Can the Subaltern Speak? Speculations on Widow Sacrifice" (1988) engages with the question of whether and how subordinated colonial peoples – Fanon's "wretched of the earth" – are able to find a voice that is truly independent from histories of oppression. The condition of **subalternity**, for Spivak, describes the inarticulacy produced by the ruling structures and society of the colonial state, which closes down possibilities of self-representation and expression.

Spivak's theorization of subalternity also intersects with a critique of anti-colonial nationalism, as the cultural practices of the artists and postcolonial intellectuals aligned with such movements have also tended to exclude the possibility of subaltern voices.

Ecocriticism

The consensus in the scientific community that the planet faces catastrophic social and environmental changes as a result of carbon emissions has had far-reaching effects in the study of the humanities over the last 30 years. In literary criticism it has led to a reassessment of the critical tradition, drawing fresh attention to the ecological aspects of the thought of numerous writers.

OUR CURRENT DESTRUCTIVE RELATIONSHIP WITH THE NATURAL WORLD RAISES QUESTIONS ABOUT HUMANITY'S ATTITUDE TOWARDS THE ENVIRONMENT THROUGHOUT HISTORY.

Particular attention has been paid to the work of natural history writers, including **Henry David Thoreau** (1817–62) and **Richard Jefferies** (1848–87). **Lawrence Buell**'s (b. 1939) *The Environmental Imagination: Thoreau, Nature Writing and the Formation of American Culture* (1995) argues for an urgent reassessment of the relationship between humanity and nature based on his close reading of Thoreau's nature writing.

Let's return to Shelley's "Defence of Poetry". Elements of his defence of the poetic imagination were closely bound up with veneration for the natural world.

THE CULTIVATION OF THOSE SCIENCES WHICH HAVE ENLARGED THE LIMITS OF THE EMPIRE OF MAN OVER THE EXTERNAL WORLD, HAS, FOR WANT OF THE POETICAL FACULTY, PROPORTIONALLY CIRCUMSCRIBED THOSE OF THE INTERNAL WORLD; AND MAN, HAVING ENSLAVED THE ELEMENTS, REMAINS HIMSELF A SLAVE.

Responding to contemporary scientific developments, Shelley articulated a view that the possibilities for human self-realization and flourishing are dependent upon a harmonious, rather than exploitative, relationship with the natural world. It was also implicit, for Shelley, that the scope of the study of poetics is far wider than, say, formal concerns with prosody.

William H. Rueckert (b. 1926) coined the term "**ecocriticism**" in his 1978 essay "Literature and Ecology: An Experiment in Ecocriticism". Thinking about how to bring together literature and ecology re-focused critical attention on the material world in the wake of the post-structuralist turn towards textuality. By attending to the specificities of place and region in literature and nature writing, ecocritics question the post-structuralist current in literary theory.

The subsequent growth of ecocriticism in the 1990s reflects the appearance of environmental politics in the 1970s and the foundation of green and ecological parties. Tensions within ecocriticism reflect divides within the wider ecological movement: some criticize a perceived anthropocentric bias in the dominant critical culture and wider society, calling attention to ways in which human consumption is privileged over the needs of the planet.

Ecocritical writing on literature has led to a reassessment of Romantic poetics, particularly the work of William Wordsworth and John Clare. **Jonathan Bate** in *Romantic Ecology: Wordsworth and the Environmental Imagination* (1991) defined the "ecopoetics" of the Romantic poets as un-political –

– OR, MORE SPECIFICALLY, PRE-POLITICAL.

This chimes with the claims of some environmentalists that the green movement transcends the ideological divides of the 20th century because of the way in which an issue such as climate change affects the human species as a species, regardless of political affiliation.

This position, however, is problematic, as it negates the status of ecocriticism as a contemporary *political* criticism with a clear ethical agenda.

Karl Kroeber's (1926–2009) *Ecological Literary Criticism: Romantic Imagining and the Biology of the Mind* (1994) similarly concentrates on re-reading the English Romantic poets, demonstrating how the modern critical tradition had neglected the presence of a proto-ecological strand in the work of Romantic writers.

THE ROMANTICS' SENSE OF RESPONSIBILITY TO NATURE AS CENTRAL TO THEIR BEING SOCIALLY VALUABLE POETS POSES DIFFICULT ISSUES OF RESPONSIBILITY FOR THEIR CRITICS. CONTEMPORARY CRITICS HAVE PREFERRED TO DWELL ON THE POETS' IDEOLOGICAL SHORTCOMINGS OR PERSONALITY QUIRKS RATHER THAN TO INQUIRE INTO THE SOCIAL RESPONSIBILITIES OF THEIR PROFESSION.

Kroeber offered a re-reading of Wordsworth's poem "Nutting" (1798), which noted a tendency in recent criticism to ignore the poem's intimate connection to the natural world, favouring psychologizing interpretations over the more literal circumstances described in the poem.

Ecocriticism does not imply any particular method of reading literature, hence the lack of consensus around how best to describe this critical tendency, which is also sometimes referred to as "green cultural studies" or "ecopoetics".

What unites ecocritics is a common focus on issues including:
- The relationship between humanity and nature
- Place consciousness
- Stewardship of the natural world.

Lawrence Buell provides a useful characterization in describing his book, *The Environmental Imagination* (1995):

[IT IS A] BROAD STUDY OF ENVIRONMENTAL PERCEPTION, THE PLACE OF NATURE IN THE HISTORY OF WESTERN THOUGHT, AND THE CONSEQUENCES FOR LITERARY SCHOLARSHIP AND INDEED FOR HUMANISTIC THOUGHT IN GENERAL OF ATTEMPTING TO IMAGINE A MORE "ECOCENTRIC" WAY OF BEING.

Concluding Remarks

The ideas and theorists surveyed here offer only a thumbnail sketch of the long history of literary criticism and theory. If the problem of representation has been prominent, this is because it is an issue of considerable aesthetic, political and philosophical importance.

Literary criticism will likely persist as a critical activity for as long as books are written, or works produced, that some choose to regard as "literature". In the 21st century, the interrelationship between "digital" and "material" culture, and the effect of this relationship on reading practices, is becoming an important question for literary critics to consider.

WHAT IS THE FUTURE OF THE BOOK? AND WHAT IS THE FUTURE OF READING?

SUCH QUESTIONS ARE INTIMATELY BOUND UP WITH THE FUTURE OF THE PLANET.

The final words go to Shelley, who reminds us that act of writing and reading literature and poetry contributes to:

Glossary

Aesthetic: that which concerns beauty or the appreciation of beauty.

Aestheticism: a 19th-century literary movement whose adherents asserted the importance of artistic autonomy from social and moral concerns, and who advocated the value of the aesthetic as an end in itself.

Allusion: an implicit reference, usually to another work of literature, a specific quotation or to a particular person or event. The use of allusion tends to presume shared knowledge between the author and reader.

Ballad: a poetic form of great antiquity, often narrating a popular tale. Material is often drawn from community life, legend or folklore.

Canon: [In relation to an individual author] the list of works accepted as being genuinely written by the author; the term usually refers to authorized (or canonized) religious writings. [In a more general sense] any group of works that are deemed to have been especially influential or important. Some would argue that universities play a major role in establishing what is regarded as a literary canon, although the boundaries of such a canon are always open to debate.

Classicism: refers to the styles, conventions, themes and modes of Classical authors, as well as their influence on later authors. Classicism in Ancient Rome meant looking to the Greeks. In 17th- and 18th-century France and England, Classicism could refer both to Greek and Roman authors.

Dialectic: a process of logical disputation that attempts to establish the truth of given conditions or opinions; a philosophical method of resolving apparent contradictions that has been influential in Western philosophy since antiquity.

Discourse (or **discursive formation**): in Foucault's terminology, the processes by which knowledge is constituted, along with the social practices, kinds of subjectivity and relations of power that are intrinsic in such kinds of knowledge. It is in discourse that knowledge and power meet.

Dithyramb: a Greek choric hymn, with mime, describing the adventures of Dionysus, the god of wine and fertility. Dithyrambic has more general connotations of "wild" song or verse.

Encomium: a formal dedication or expression of praise.

Essay: a genre of writing, usually short and in prose, which is often used in literary criticism and which addresses itself to a particular topic or variety of topics. It derives from the French verb "*essayer*" (to attempt). The word was coined by the French writer **Michel de Montaigne** (1533–92) in his *Essais* (1580). The essays of **Francis Bacon** (1561–1626) were influential in disseminating the genre in English.

Hermeneutic: concerning interpretation, particularly with regard to Scripture or literary texts.

Heroic couplets: a common metrical form in English poetry, consisting of rhymed decasyllables, usually written in iambic pentameter.

Heteronormativity: a view of sexuality that falsely universalizes heterosexual experience.

Humanism: a philosophical outlook that prioritizes human, as against divine, matters, tending to regard humans as essentially rational, responsible and progressive beings.

Metaphor: the application of a name or descriptive phrase to an object to which it is imaginatively rather than literally applicable. For example, the "wine-dark sea" in Homer's *Odyssey*.

Mimesis: from the Greek for "imitation" (as in mime), which also carries the sense of literary representation.

Neoclassicism: a literary or artistic movement seeking to bring about the revival of **classical** style and forms. In England, the dates of this fall roughly between 1660 and 1780. The literature of this period is sometimes referred to as Augustan literature.

Objectivism: a philosophical position that states the cosmos is determined by laws of causality that can be observed and delineated through observation. Human actions are not free because they are determined by these external laws.

Oeuvre: the works of an author or artist regarded collectively or as a whole.

Phenomenology: the philosophical study of structures of experience and consciousness.

Relativism: a philosophical stance which holds that all truths are relative to the individual and are thus not absolute.

Subaltern: in postcolonial studies, this concept refers to social groups that are excluded from the hegemonic power structures of colony and metropole. See, in particular, the work of the Subaltern Studies Group.

Subjectivism: a philosophical position that asserts human freedom from external determination, foregrounding the active role of consciousness (subjectivity) in generating the phenomenal world.

Teleology: the explanation of phenomena with reference to the purpose or end served, rather than the cause.

Textuality: interpretation characterized by strict adherence to the text; also the quality of written, as opposed to spoken, language.

Further Reading

Atherton, Carol, *Defining Literary Criticism: Scholarship, Authority and the Possession of Literary Knowledge, 1880–2002* (London: Palgrave, 2005).

Bressler, Charles E., *Literary Criticism: An Introduction to Theory and Practice*, 5th edn (London: Longman, 2011).

Day, Gary, *Literary Criticism: A New History* (Edinburgh: Edinburgh University Press, 2010).

Donovan, Josephine, ed., *Feminist Literary Criticism: Explorations in Theory* (Lexington: University Press of Kentucky, 1975).

Eagleton, Mary, ed., *Feminist Literary Criticism* (Harlow: Longman, 1991).

Eagleton, Terry, *Literary Theory: An Introduction*, 2nd edn (Oxford: Blackwell, 1996).

------, *Marxism and Literary Criticism* (London: Methuen, 1976).

Ellman, Maud, ed., *Psychoanalytic Literary Criticism* (London: Longman, 1994).

Habib, M.A.R., *A History of Literary Criticism and Theory, from Plato to the Present* (Oxford: Blackwell, 2007).

Leitch, Vincent B., *Literary Criticism in the 21st Century: Theory Renaissance* (London: Bloomsbury, 2014).

Plain, Gill and Susan Sellers, eds, *A History of Feminist Literary Criticism* (Cambridge: Cambridge University Press, 2007).

Richards, I.A., *Principles of Literary Criticism* (London: Kegan Paul, Trench, Trubner and Co., 1925).

Russell, D.A. and Michael Winterbottom, eds, *Classical Literary Criticism* (Oxford: Oxford University Press, 1989).

Wimsatt, Jr., William K. and Cleanth Brooks, *Literary Criticism: A Short History* (London: Routledge and Kegan Paul, 1957).

Owen Holland completed a doctorate in Criticism and Culture in 2015. He studied in the Cambridge University Faculty of English where he also taught classes in the history of literary criticism and practical criticism. He has published work in the *New Theatre Quarterly*, the *Journal of William Morris Studies*, *Social History* and elsewhere.

Piero is an illustrator, artist and graphic designer whose work has been included in the Royal College of Art in London. He has illustrated many Introducing titles. pieroart@gmail.com

Index